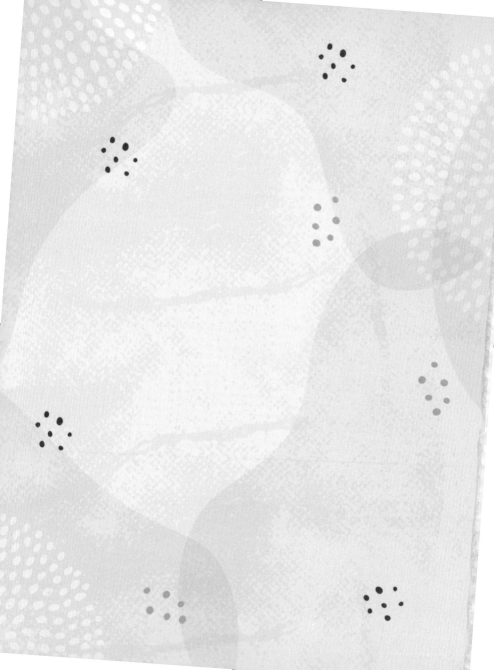

GOD MADE YOU FOR MORE

MariLee Parrish

GOD MADE YOU FOR MORE

Devotions and Prayers for Girls

BARBOUR **kidz**

A Division of Barbour Publishing

HELLO, MY FRIEND!

I'm excited to walk through the Bible with you from beginning to end, talking about at least one scripture from every book in the whole Bible. I've even had a little help from my daughter, who just happens to be your age. Jessa is really good at telling me if something I've written makes sense to an eight-to-twelve-year-old and sharing her own perspective at times!

God's Word has so much to say about the amazing plans He has for your life. It's our prayer that as you read these words each day, three important things will happen:

1. *You'll find out how much God loves you.*

2. *You'll see and believe the awesome plans He has for you.*

3. *You'll develop a deeper love for God and His Word in the process.*

With love and prayers for God to shower His blessings on you as you grow up,

MariLee (and Jessa too!)

Jesus, we ask that Your Spirit would come alive in the heart of each girl who picks up this book. Let Your words and Your love for them change their whole life. In Your all-powerful name we pray. Amen.

LET'S START AT THE BEGINNING

*In the beginning God made from nothing
the heavens and the earth.*
GENESIS 1:1 NLV

. . . .

The book of Genesis is the very first book in the Bible, and it contains a couple thousand years of history! In it we see how God created the world, and we meet Adam and Eve, Noah, Abraham, Isaac, Jacob, Joseph, and many other real people who followed God. Why are these people who lived so long ago so important to us now? Check out what Jesus has to say about this in Luke 24:27 (NIV): "And beginning with Moses and all the Prophets, he explained to them what was said in all the Scriptures concerning himself." Jesus seems to be saying here that every scripture all the way back to the very beginning points to Him! And this little devotional is intended to do just that: point you to Jesus.

So we're starting at the beginning to learn what God has to say about your life and His great plans for you. He absolutely made you for more than you could ever imagine!

*Creator God, thank You for Your Word.
I'm eager to learn more about You and
to see how I fit into Your plan.*

7

MADE iN HiS IMAGE

And God made man in His own likeness. In the likeness
of God He made him. He made both male and female.
And God wanted good to come to them. . . . God saw
all that He had made and it was very good.
GENESIS 1:27–28, 31 NLV

Do you have any siblings? Do you look like them a little bit? Maybe you have the same hair color or freckles. What about your mom and dad? Do you resemble them in some way? Families come in all shapes and sizes. You may not all look similar, but you probably have at least some characteristics that are alike. It's not just a physical appearance kind of thing. We often resemble the people we're around the most, even in terms of personality. For example, if your mom has a great sense of humor, the people in your family probably appreciate laughter. You might be funny just like her!

God says He made each of us in His own image. He looks at you and says that He did a good job. Think about some of the character traits of God. How do you personally resemble Him?

Heavenly Father, thank You for making me in Your
image! I want to resemble You in lots of ways!

SPECIAL THINGS ABOUT GOD

*And he passed in front of Moses, proclaiming, "The LORD,
the LORD, the compassionate and gracious God, slow
to anger, abounding in love and faithfulness. . . ."*
EXODUS 34:6 NIV

The book of Exodus shows us how God guides and rescues His people. He did it then and still does it today. God prepared Moses for a very specific job, and He stayed with Moses every step of the way. Even when Moses disobeyed God, God was still loving and full of grace. Yep, he still faced consequences for disobedience just like you probably do when your parents discipline you. But God worked everything out for good.

Is God preparing you for a life of purpose and adventure too? You bet He is! So here's what you can do about it right now: get to know God by reading His Word and talking with Him in prayer. He promises to be with you and guide you every day of your life! Today's verse tells us some special things about God. What are they?

*Lord God, I'm excited to be on this adventure
with You because You are so kind and good.*

YOU CAN BELONG TO GOD

"Be holy to Me, for I the Lord am holy. I have divided you from the nations, so you belong to Me."
LEVITICUS 20:26 NLV

. . . .

Leviticus can seem like a strange book. What's with all those rules? But this seemingly strange book of the Bible tells us something very important. God is holy and He hates sin. In Old Testament Bible times, God's people had to sacrifice animals so that God would forgive their disobedience. They had to do this over and over and over again when they sinned. That's why God sent Jesus. He died on the cross for our sins because He was the only perfect sacrifice who could take care of our sin once and for all. Through Jesus' sacrifice of Himself, God made a way for you to belong to Him. Jesus is the only way that any of us can have a relationship with a holy God.

Dear God, I am sorry for my sins, and I understand that You are holy. I want to belong to You. I believe that Jesus died on the cross to make a way for me to be made right with You. Please forgive my sins and come into my heart and make me more like You.

If you've prayed this prayer, make sure to talk to your parents or a trusted grown-up about this life-changing decision!

ROAD TRIPS

"May the Lord bring good to you and keep you. May the Lord make His face shine upon you, and be kind to you. May the Lord show favor toward you, and give you peace."
NUMBERS 6:24–26 NLV

Do you and your family enjoy road trips? Some families love to get to their destination as fast as possible. Some enjoy the journey and all the stops on the way. Have you ever been on a road trip that lasted way longer than it was supposed to? Maybe you got a flat tire or had to make too many potty stops?

Numbers is a book about a trip too. God's people were on a journey that should have taken two weeks but ended up taking forty years! That's one crazy road trip! God's people kept disobeying and sinning against Him. So they wandered around in the desert for an unreasonably long time instead of trusting in God and reaching their destination successfully.

What can you learn from this book in the Bible? Follow God with your whole heart and trust Him no matter what. Don't let unbelief keep you from enjoying God's blessings.

Lord, I'm beginning to see that You made me for more than a boring life of unbelief. Help me follow You faithfully.

11

GUIDELINES FOR THE JOURNEY

"And you must love the Lord your God with all your heart and with all your soul and with all your strength. Keep these words in your heart that I am telling you today. Do your best to teach them to your children."
DEUTERONOMY 6:5–7 NLV

. . . .

The older generation that had wandered in the desert was gone and the new generation was getting ready to enter the Promised Land. Their parents hadn't trusted God very well, so Moses had to teach them about God and His commands and promises. This is what's happening in the book of Deuteronomy. The Ten Commandments are given, and Moses teaches the people that God rewards obedience but enforces consequences for sin, just like any good parent does.

Today's scripture provides great guidelines for your journey with God: love Him and obey Him and teach your children to do the same. This world will throw a lot of mixed-up ideas into your path, but if you faithfully follow the Lord, you will be blessed and so will your descendants!

Lord, thank You that I have Your Word to follow and obey and that Your Spirit is alive in my heart to help me on the journey.

GOD IS WITH YOU

"Have I not told you? Be strong and have strength of heart! Do not be afraid or lose faith. For the Lord your God is with you anywhere you go."
JOSHUA 1:9 NLV

. . . .

Have you heard the old Sunday school song "Joshua Fought the Battle of Jericho"? If not, ask one of your parents or church leaders to sing it to you. It'll probably get stuck in your head for a while! We learn in that song and in the book of Joshua that the walls came tumbling down. Why? Because Joshua obeyed God even when God asked him to do something that sounded a bit crazy! The book of Joshua shows that God is all-powerful and works on behalf of His people. Want to see something really cool? Go look up Joshua 10:13–14 in your Bible. Wow!

Today's scripture is a reminder that God is with you everywhere you go. He can do miracles on your behalf. You can trust Him with your whole heart!

Wow, God! You are amazing! I'm so glad You love me and are with me always. Give me courage to follow You all the days of my life!

GOD VALUES WOMEN

Now Lappidoth's wife Deborah, a woman who spoke
for God, was judging Israel at that time. She would
sit under the tree. . . . And the people of Israel came
to her to find out what was right or wrong.
JUDGES 4:4–5 NLV

- -

The book of Judges tells the history of the Israelites over a period of about three hundred years. Guess what they did during that time? They would obey God for a while and follow His plan and receive His blessing. Then they would forget God, do whatever they wanted, and become miserable. And they repeated that cycle over and over.

Deborah was a wise, God-fearing woman. She became one of the judges over all of Israel. Many people went to her to hear her advice. She urged the Israelites to repent and turn back to God. We can learn from Deborah that God greatly values women and uses women in ministry. God set up Deborah as a judge over all of the Jewish people, not just other women. She even commanded an army to go into battle, and God gave them victory.

Just as He did for Deborah, God has great plans for your life and made you a special girl on purpose!

Lord, help me follow Deborah's example and
look to You for courage and wisdom.

THE TRUST FALL

But Ruth said, "Do not beg me to leave you or turn away from following you. I will go where you go. I will live where you live. Your people will be my people. And your God will be my God."
RUTH 1:16 NLV

• •

The book of Ruth is a story of God using three people who were faithful to Him during a very dark time in the world. Ruth decided to put her trust in the one true God, and God blessed her because of it. Life wasn't easy for Ruth, but God was with her. God used her family line throughout history, and eventually Jesus was born from the descendants of Ruth and Boaz!

Let's play a little game. Ask your mom or dad to play along. With your back turned toward them, ask your parent to catch you when you fall backward. This is called a trust fall. Do you actually trust your parent to catch you? Try this a few times. Did they catch you every time? I sure hope so! God promises to be faithful to you too. Just like Ruth, you can trust Him no matter what.

Lord, help me trust You like Ruth did!

THE INSIDE

But the Lord said to Samuel, "Do not look at the way
he looks on the outside. . . . For the Lord does not look
at the things man looks at. A man looks at the outside
of a person, but the Lord looks at the heart."
1 SAMUEL 16:7 NLV

God started speaking to Samuel when he was just a young boy. God asked him to do many hard things, but he learned to trust God and listen to His voice.

One time when God was speaking, He told Samuel not to judge people by their appearance. This lesson is an important one to carry with you as you grow up. You were made for more than just to look good on the outside. God looks at your heart. Do things look just as nice in there as they do on the outside? Ask God to make your heart clean, and decide today that you won't judge other people by what they look like. Kindness and love on the inside can make anyone beautiful.

Lord, forgive me for judging people by their outward
appearance. Please make my heart beautiful and
help me look for that beauty inside others.

REPENTANCE AND FORGIVENESS

"For this reason You are great, O Lord God. There is none like You. And there is no God but You, by all that we have heard with our ears."
2 Samuel 7:22 nlv

• •

In the second book of Samuel, David becomes the king of Israel. We learn of his life and his adventures as a great warrior. But David also made some really bad choices and sinned greatly against God. David was genuinely sorry for his sins, though, and he repented. To repent means to ask God for forgiveness and also turn away from that sin and go in a different direction. Even though David suffered the consequences of his sin, God forgave him and kept His promises to him. Jesus, our Savior, would eventually come from David's family line.

Have you ever made a bad choice and felt like God was trying to tell you something? Listen to the voice in your heart. God will let you know if you need to repent and ask forgiveness and then turn in a new direction.

Lord God, help me to listen for Your voice
and then do what You ask of me.

17

OBEYING GOD

*He said, "O Lord, God of Israel, there is no God like You
in heaven above or on earth below. You are keeping Your
agreement and are showing loving-kindness to Your
servants who walk in Your ways with all their heart."*
1 KINGS 8:23 NLV

King Solomon was one of the greatest kings in history. His dad was King David. Solomon was a wise and honorable king for many years. He spent seven years building the special temple for God. He praised God before all of the people of Israel and thanked Him for keeping His promises. Later in his life, though, Solomon disobeyed God. Disobedience to God always causes all kinds of problems. The consequences of Solomon's actions were severe.

Like King Solomon, you were made for more than living with the sadness and shame of disobedience. Think about today's verse: God is faithful and good. He is loving and kind and you will be blessed if you follow Him with all your heart.

Lord, there is no one like You! Thank You for Your
Spirit who is alive in me, who helps me to walk in
Your ways. Keep me close to Your heart, Lord Jesus.

FAITH IN THE UNSEEN

*He answered, "Do not be afraid. For those who are
with us are more than those who are with them." Then
Elisha prayed and said, "O Lord, I pray, open his eyes,
that he may see." And the Lord opened the servant's
eyes, and he saw. He saw that the mountain was full of
horses and war-wagons of fire all around Elisha.*
2 Kings 6:16–17 NLV

This is one of the coolest stories in the Bible! Go read the entire story in 2 Kings 6. And it's not just a story—it really happened.

Faith is believing in things that are unseen. The Bible tells us God has placed angels around us to protect us and watch over us. Take a few minutes to look up these scriptures in your Bible:

- Hebrews 11:1
- Matthew 18:10
- Psalm 103:20
- Revelation 5:11–12

What do you think God wants you to know about "things unseen"? God made you for more than what your eyes can see!

Lord, the stories in the Bible are truly amazing!
I believe You can do anything. You work
miracles and are all-powerful. I'm so grateful
You love me and want what's best for me.

19

LOOK TO GOD

"Is not the Lord your God with you? Has He not given you peace on every side? For He has given the people of the land into my hand. The land is put under my rule before the Lord and His people. Now set your heart and soul to look to the Lord your God."
1 Chronicles 22:18–19 nlv

- -

In 1 Chronicles, we learn more about the life and reign of King David. At the end of the book, David makes arrangements to build God's special temple. He ordered all of Israel's leaders to help his son Solomon build it after his death. God made some special promises to King David, and He kept them all.

King David loved God and led his people in true worship. His life shows us that we can walk with God and have a close relationship with Him. King David instructed the people, "Set your heart and soul to look to the Lord your God." What do you picture when you hear those words? Can you set your heart and soul to look to God too?

Lord, I want to follow You wholeheartedly,
the way King David did.

GOOD KiNGS AND BAD KiNGS

*"If My people who are called by My name put away
their pride and pray, and look for My face, and turn
from their sinful ways, then I will hear from heaven.
I will forgive their sin, and will heal their land."*
2 CHRONICLES 7:14 NLV

As the second book of Chronicles begins, the new king, Solomon, builds the temple. Israel prospered during Solomon's reign. But Solomon chose to sin against God too. God came to Solomon and told him that the people needed to humble themselves and turn away from their bad choices. If they did, God would forgive them and heal their land.

The rest of Chronicles is about a bunch of different kings, some good and some bad. The good kings honored God and experienced His blessing. The bad kings did not. At the end of the book, the people had abandoned God, the temple was destroyed, and the Israelites were conquered by a foreign power.

It's a sad ending that could have been prevented if God's people had just obeyed Him. God knows and wants what is best for us.

Lord, I believe You know what is best for me. Thank
You that I have the Holy Spirit to help me obey You.

GOD CAN USE YOU

"O Lord God of Israel, You are right and good. For some of us have been left alive to return, as it is this day. See, we are guilty before You. No one can stand before You because of this."
EZRA 9:15 NLV

· ·

In the book of Ezra, we learn more about God's faithfulness to His people, even after they had sinned against Him time and time again. God's people finally got to go back to their homeland in Jerusalem after being held in captivity by the Babylonians for seventy years. God used Ezra and another leader to lead the people back home and rebuild the temple.

What can you learn from the book of Ezra? Even when things look hopeless, God can still use you. If you've messed up big, talk to God about it. Because of Jesus and all He has done for you, you can go right up to God's throne confidently (Hebrews 4:16) and talk to Him about anything.

> Lord, I confess my sins to You. I've messed up. I'd still like You to use me, Lord. Would You help me get back on the right path?

GO TO GOD FIRST

Ezra said to them, "Go, eat and drink what you enjoy, and give some to him who has nothing ready. For this day is holy to our Lord. Do not be sad for the joy of the Lord is your strength."
NEHEMIAH 8:10 NLV

• •

Nehemiah loved God and he loved to pray. He prayed a lot for God's people. He wanted them to learn to love and honor God too. He kept praying for that to happen. Nehemiah knew that obeying God joyfully was the key to success and strength. He was a good leader and motivated the people to rebuild the walls around Jerusalem that helped prevent God's temple from being attacked.

One important thing we can learn from both Ezra and Nehemiah is to go to God first. When either of these men had a problem or a question or needed advice, they prayed about it first. Ask God for help to make prayer a regular habit in your life too.

Lord, instead of going to everyone else for
help or trying to make things happen on
my own, teach me to come to You first.

COURAGE AND STRENGTH

*"For if you keep quiet at this time, help will come
to the Jews from another place. But you and your
father's house will be destroyed. Who knows if you
have not become queen for such a time as this?"*
ESTHER 4:14 NLV

The story of the orphan Jewish girl who became queen sounds like a fairy tale, right? The awesome thing is that it's a true story! God used Esther greatly to change the heart of a king and save an entire nation of people. The king's evil adviser, Haman, was determined to kill all the Jews in the kingdom. God gave Esther courage to stand up to evil, even if it might cost her her life. He helped her do and say the right thing at just the right time, and He can do the same for you!

Are you in a situation that's going to require some courage? Take some time right now to ask God to give you strength and wisdom. He loves to hear your prayers!

Lord, I believe You made me for more than I
can ever imagine. Please give me the courage
and strength to follow Your plan for my life.

RESPOND IN WORSHIP

"But as for me, I know that the One Who bought
me and made me free from sin lives, and that
He will stand upon the earth in the end."
JOB 19:25 NLV

. . . .

We can learn a lot from what happened to Job. Job was a rich guy who loved God. But sadly, he lost nearly everything. His wife and his friends even turned against him. And guess what Job's response was. "The LORD gave me what I had, and the LORD has taken it away. Praise the name of the LORD!" (Job 1:21 NLT).

After all that bad stuff happened, Job worshipped! Can you imagine having the worst day of your entire life and then praising God? That's exactly what Job did. Job still trusted God, and God blessed him greatly in the end.

Job knew that God saw him. And just like Job, we can know that God is always with us, even when we're having a bad day, a bad week, or a bad year!

Lord, like Job says, I know that You're the
One who bought me and made me free
from sin. My life is Yours. I trust You with it.
Help me to praise You no matter what.

HE MAKES US STRONG

The Lord is my Shepherd. I will have everything I need. He lets me rest in fields of green grass. He leads me beside the quiet waters. He makes me strong again. He leads me in the way of living right with Himself which brings honor to His name.
PSALM 23:1–3 NLV

• •

We're going to spend a few days here in the Psalms. Psalms is an awesome book of honest worship in the Bible. King David is known to have written many of the psalms. He had a lot of good and bad things happen to him in his lifetime, and he wrote songs about many of those experiences. He poured out his heart to God in those songs.

My daughter Jessa broke two bones in her leg this past fall. The injury took her out for over three months! We spent a lot of time praying for God to heal those bones and strengthen her muscles. Slowly but surely, God healed her body. We trusted that God would make Jessa strong again.

Lord, we worship You with songs of praise!
We are so thankful that You are the God
who leads us and makes us strong. Thank
You for giving us everything we need.

26

PRAISE ACTIVITY

He says, "Be still, and know that I am God; I will be exalted among the nations, I will be exalted in the earth."
PSALM 46:10 NIV

• •

Let's do a little activity today. Get out a piece of paper or a journal and write out today's scripture verse. Read it over five times in a row (that's an easy way to help memorize it!). Now, can you write a prayer to God in your own words using this verse? *Exalt* means to praise God and lift Him high. Can you think of reasons to praise God? Write them down. Then draw a picture to go along with what you've written.

Using these ideas is a great way to spend time with God throughout the book of Psalms or any part of the Bible. God wants to speak to you in many different ways. Are you listening for Him?

God, I praise You for being an awesome and good God. You are the Creator of the whole world, and yet You still care deeply about me! Help me to be still before You and to take time to pray and worship. I love You, Lord.

KNOW THE WAY TO GO

Your Word is a lamp to my feet and a light to my path.
PSALM 119:105 NLV

. . . .

Do you have a night-light in your bedroom or hallway? It helps to have a little bit of light in the darkness, doesn't it? It's hard to know which way to go when it's completely dark, especially if you have to get up in the night to go to the bathroom. But that little bulb in a night-light provides just enough light for you to see. God's Word is like that. When you're struggling with what to do in life or you have a problem you can't figure out, God's words in the Bible can help you get on the right path, just like a night-light helps you see in the dark.

Let's try our praise activity again. Write out Psalm 119:105 along with a prayer of praise. Can you draw a picture of God's Word being a lamp in the dark?

Lord, thank You for being my light in the
dark. I'm glad You've given us Your words
to help us know which way to go.

COMPLETELY KNOWN BY GOD

*Your eyes saw me before I was put together. And all the days of
my life were written in Your book before any of them came to be.*
Psalm 139:16 nlv

• •

God's Word tells us that He knew you before you were even born. He knows everything about you and loves you so very much! He knows everything you think and everything you're going to do. Is that kind of hard to believe? The author of Psalm 139 thought so too. He said, "Your knowledge is amazing to me. It is more than I can understand" (verse 6 icb).

Allow this message from God to wash over your heart: God loves you. He sees you. He wants a relationship with you. You are His beloved. You matter to God.

Read Psalm 139:1–16 today and pick out your favorite verse to write down in your journal. What picture will you draw to go along with it?

> Lord, let Your love change me. I'm beginning
> to see how much I matter to You and how You
> made me for more than I can even imagine.
> It's hard to believe You know everything about
> me and love me anyway. Thank You, God!

WISDOM FOR LIFE

*Trust in the Lord with all your heart, and do not trust
in your own understanding. Agree with Him in all your
ways, and He will make your paths straight.*
PROVERBS 3:5–6 NLV

. . . .

Can kids have wisdom? You bet they can! Kids who love and follow Jesus can be very wise! In fact, there's a verse in 1 Timothy that says not to let anyone look down on you because you're young but to set a wise example for others instead (4:12).

The book of Proverbs gives us a lot of advice for living a wise and godly life. We can't just become wise on our own—that would be trusting in our own understanding. We need help from the Holy Spirit. Proverbs reminds us how great and good God is. It gives us excellent advice for life and friendships and helps us turn away from the things of this world that are not good for followers of Jesus.

God has awesome plans for your life, and He can help you be a wise kid if you ask Him and do what He says!

Lord, please help me to be a wise kid.
Show me Your ways and help me know the
right thing to do in each situation.

A PURE HEART

Keep your heart pure for out of it are the important things of life.
PROVERBS 4:23 NLV

• •

Sometimes it's a good idea to look up scriptures in other versions of the Bible. Seeing a verse worded in several different ways can help us better understand the full meaning of the verse. Take a look at Proverbs 4:23 in a few other versions:

The International Children's Bible says, "Be very careful about what you think. Your thoughts run your life." *The Message* says, "Keep vigilant watch over your heart; that's where life starts." The New International Version says, "Above all else, guard your heart, for everything you do flows from it." And the Amplified Bible says, "Watch over your heart with all diligence, for from it flow the springs of life."

What do you think God wants you to know about keeping your heart pure? Take a few minutes to ask God about that in prayer. Write down anything you hear God say to you about it.

Lord God, I want to do what You say and keep my heart pure. Having a pure heart is very important to You, so I want it to be important to me too. Help me to listen for Your voice and do what You say.

31

A GOD-SHAPED HOLE

*He has made everything beautiful in its time. He has put thoughts
of the forever in man's mind, yet man cannot understand
the work God has done from the beginning to the end.*
ECCLESIASTES 3:11 NLV

. . . .

The New International Version puts Ecclesiastes 3:11 a little differently: "He has also set eternity in the human heart." The book of Ecclesiastes contains some great wisdom for a girl who knows she's made for more. The author wants us to know that earthly things are only temporary and will never fill our hearts with joy. Only God can do that! Right at the very beginning, when you were being formed in your mother's womb, He set eternity in your heart. It's like a God-shaped hole that you'll only ever be able to fill with God Himself. People try all kinds of other things to fill up that hole, but it just never works out.

As you grow up, remember not to make any "thing" more important than God.

Lord, thank You for filling the hole in my heart! I
know true happiness can never come from things.
I'm so glad my joy comes from knowing You.

WISDOM FOR RELATIONSHIPS

Place me like a seal over your heart, like a seal on your arm.
SONG OF SOLOMON 8:6 NIV

. . . .

Song of Solomon is a book of the Bible that's actually a poem about married love and God's plan for marriage. You'll probably read this book more when you're a grown-up. Marriage is a special gift that God has planned for a man and a woman. When you get married, you are actually entering into a covenant before God by pledging to love someone else for the rest of their life. A covenant is a special promise you make with God. It's a really big deal.

As you grow up, be on the lookout for what God wants to show you about a future husband. Also be praying for wisdom as special friends come into your life. If you seek God in all your decisions, you can trust that He will help you choose wisely in all your relationships.

Lord, I want to come to You first when I make decisions about any kind of friends I allow in my life. Help me to be wise and to listen to Your will for me.

A GOOD FATHER

Come, people of Jacob. Let us walk in the light of the Lord.
ISAIAH 2:5 NLV

God used prophets like Isaiah to give special messages to the people of Israel. Isaiah had to tell God's people a lot of things. First, he had to tell them that they weren't making good choices. They needed to be sorry for the way they were acting and change their ways. That's what repentance means. Isaiah warned them that if they didn't repent, they would suffer even more consequences for their sin.

God told Isaiah that He was sad that His children weren't obeying (Isaiah 1:1–19) and that they were experiencing punishment that they brought on themselves by not following God's plan. The people wanted their own way again, and bad things were happening because of it.

But then Isaiah also gave them a message of hope: Jesus was coming! The Savior of the whole world! The answer to the problem of sin was going to come and make everything right. God promised He would bless His children and give them another chance. God is a good Father—the best! He knows exactly what His children need.

Thank You, Lord. You are a good Father.

EVERYTHING YOU NEED

*For to us a Child will be born. To us a Son will be given.
And the rule of the nations will be on His shoulders.
His name will be called Wonderful, Teacher, Powerful
God, Father Who Lives Forever, Prince of Peace.*
ISAIAH 9:6 NLV

- -

The book of Isaiah has so much to teach us! For a girl who is made for more, this beautiful book gives wisdom and hope for all situations. Isaiah urged God's people to repent and turn back to God. That's wisdom to tuck in your heart for your entire life.

Isaiah also tells of the coming Savior! This Savior, Jesus, would change everything. And that is still true today. Jesus is everything your heart needs: a Savior, a Teacher, a Counselor, a Father. . .and He is peace.

What is your heart in need of today? Turn to Jesus and let Him fill you with everything you need.

Lord God, I come to You and give You my whole heart. Show me anything in my life that doesn't match up with the great plan You have for me. Help me to repent and follow Your ways instead.

GOD SPEAKS

Whether you turn to the right or to the left, your ears will hear a voice behind you, saying, "This is the way; walk in it."
ISAIAH 30:21 NIV

. . . .

Do you believe God still speaks to people today? Think of some of the ways He communicates with us. We know He still speaks through His Word. He can speak through pastors and teachers. He speaks through His creation. He can speak through songs and other people. The Bible tells us He even spoke through a donkey once (check out Numbers 22:21–39)! What does that tell us about how God speaks? It tells us that God can speak to us however He wants to!

Are you taking the time to listen? When you pray, are you just sending your wish list to heaven, or are you having a conversation? Try getting in the habit of doing more listening in prayer and less talking. Let's try it right now. Read today's scripture and then ask God what He wants you to know about this verse. Sit in silence for a while and wait for God. He might surprise you with what He has to say!

Lord, I believe You want me to know Your voice.
Help me recognize You when You're speaking to me.

A LITTLE MIXED UP

*But they who wait upon the Lord will get new strength.
They will rise up with wings like eagles. They will run and
not get tired. They will walk and not become weak.*
Isaiah 40:31 NLV

· ·

The Bible has a bunch of sayings like this: Wait and get new strength. Walk and don't get tired. Trade your ashes for beauty. Lose your life to gain it. These sound a little mixed up, right? But it's actually what the Christian life is all about: faith.

When you trust God even when you don't understand and even when something doesn't seem to make sense, He will always come through for you. He loves to show Himself to His people. He wants you to know how close He is. He wants you to know that He sees you and is working on your behalf.

Lord, I choose to trust You even when things don't
make sense to me. Thank You for seeing me and
knowing what I need. Thank You for showing me that
You made me for more than what my eyes can see.

NEVER ALONE

"Do not fear, for I am with you. Do not be afraid, for I am your God. I will give you strength, and for sure I will help you. Yes, I will hold you up with My right hand that is right and good."
ISAIAH 41:10 NLV

. . . .

Do you enjoy being alone? Some kids enjoy a bit of quiet time now and then. Some kids need it. Others want to be with people all the time and fill their beds with as many stuffed animals as possible because they never want to feel alone, not even when they're sleeping. No matter which type of kid you are, God promises that He will never leave you! He is with you always. Even when the lights go out after your parents have tucked you in bed, God is with you still. You are never alone.

God, knowing You are always with me makes my heart so happy. Thank You that I don't have to feel loneliness or fear, because You will never leave me.

WHAT JESUS DID FOR YOU

But He was hurt for our wrong-doing. He was crushed
for our sins. He was punished so we would have
peace. He was beaten so we would be healed.
ISAIAH 53:5 NLV

. . . .

God is holy and perfect in all of His ways. We are not. We sin. We mess up. We've all made lots of mistakes. We can't understand everything about God and His ways, but we do know that we can't get to God if we aren't perfect. That's why Jesus came! God made us and loves us so much. But He made each of us with the ability to make our own choices. We can choose to live in our sins, forever separated from God. Or we can choose to accept the righteousness (perfect-ness) of Jesus and be with God for eternity.

Jesus died to take our sins so that when God looks at us, instead of seeing our sinfulness, He sees the perfect sacrifice that Jesus made for us. Jesus came and died so that we could be made perfect before God. It was the only way.

I'm so thankful You took the punishment for my
sins, Jesus. Help me live my life to honor You.

HOPE FROM JESUS

The Spirit of the Lord God is on me, because the Lord has chosen me to bring good news to poor people. He has sent me to heal those with a sad heart. He has sent me to tell those who are being held and those in prison that they can go free.
ISAIAH 61:1 NLV

. . . .

Jesus Himself quoted these words from Isaiah in Luke 4:18–19. Jesus came to heal people with hurting hearts and to set people free. He's not just talking about physical conditions like people who need healing from an illness or people who are in jail. He's talking about people with broken hearts and those who are stuck in fear. Jesus came to bring hope to anyone who needed it. Isaiah foretold this about Jesus.

Do you need hope or healing? You can find it in Jesus. Ask Jesus to show you how He can use *you* to bring His hope to hurting people too. He'll point you in the right direction and give you courage as you go.

Jesus, You are the hope of the world and the hope of my heart. Show me how I can spread Your hope to everyone around me.

HOPE FOR THE FUTURE

"For I know the plans I have for you," declares the Lord,
"plans to prosper you and not to harm you, plans to give
you hope and a future. Then you will call on me and come
and pray to me, and I will listen to you. You will seek me
and find me when you seek me with all your heart."
JEREMIAH 29:11–13 NIV

• •

Jeremiah was a prophet who had to deliver some bad news. Nobody liked him. Nobody listened to him at all. Not his friends. Not even his own family. But even when he felt alone, Jeremiah obeyed God and kept on telling the people that they needed to repent and turn back to God.

When the prophets had bad news to deliver, God always gave them hope. Verse 14 (NIV) continues, " 'I will be found by you,' declares the Lord, 'and will bring you back from captivity.' "

You can find hope in these words too. God wants you to find Him and know Him personally. He wants you to know you are never alone and that He made you for more!

Lord God, thank You for giving me hope for the
future. I'm so glad You are with me, always!

41

THE BEST PARENT EVER

*Because of the LORD's great love we are not
consumed, for his compassions never fail. They are
new every morning; great is your faithfulness.*
LAMENTATIONS 3:22–23 NIV

God is the very best Parent. The book of Lamentations shows us more about that. Just as a good parent would do, God warned His children what would happen if they disobeyed. Are you noticing a recurring theme? God wanted His kids to listen so that they wouldn't have to suffer painful consequences. His heart hurts when His children disobey.

Isaiah 30:18 (ICB) says, "The Lord wants to show his mercy to you. He wants to rise and comfort you. The Lord is a fair God. And everyone who waits for his help will be happy."

God's desire is to shower you with love and compassion. He longs for you to let Him bless you. Everything that happens to you in this life can be used for your good and God's glory (see Romans 8:28). Imagine a parent who loves you unconditionally and never ever makes a mistake. That's who God is.

Thank You for being such a good Father,
Lord! I choose to come to You each day,
knowing You want the very best for me.

A NEW HEART

"I will give you a new heart and put a new spirit within you. I will take away your heart of stone and give you a heart of flesh."
EZEKIEL 36:26 NLV

. . . .

Ezekiel was a prophet and preacher to God's people while they were held captive in Babylon. He was told to deliver the same message that Jeremiah had given: *Repent, guys! Turn back to God!*

God promised to allow some of His children to go back to their homeland and have a fresh start, obeying God and receiving a new heart and spirit. They needed to be taught about true worship: getting their eyes off themselves and on God.

When you commit your life to Christ, He gives you a new heart and a new spirit too. God removes your old stubborn and sinful heart and gives you a soft and tender heart that wants to worship Jesus and follow His ways.

Lord God, thank You so much for my
new heart. Help me to take my eyes off
myself and learn how to worship You.

PEER PRESSURE AND FRIENDSHIPS

*"Those who are wise will shine like the bright heavens.
And those who lead many to do what is right and
good will shine like the stars forever and ever."*
DANIEL 12:3 NLV

• •

Daniel was a young guy who was held captive in Babylon with his friends. He trusted in God and obeyed His commands. You've probably heard about this famous man, right? Daniel in the lions' den? Daniel's friends thrown into a fiery furnace? God was with them through some seemingly impossible times! These friends remained faithful to God even when those around them didn't follow God at all.

Do you know what peer pressure is? It's when the people around you heavily influence your decisions. Lots of kids (and even grown-ups) end up making decisions to fit in with their friends.

Peer pressure can be rough, but God can give you special courage just like He gave Daniel and his friends. God can help you find other friends who follow Him too.

Lord, I need some help finding good friends who follow You. Please give me courage to make good decisions, even if some of my friends aren't. I want You to be the most important influence in my life.

44

LOVE AND WORSHIP

*"I want loving-kindness and not a gift to be given in worship.
I want people to know God instead of giving burnt gifts."*
HOSEA 6:6 NLV

In the book of Hosea, God again shows unfailing love for His sinful and disobedient people. This is the message you will hear all throughout the Bible. Acts 3:19 (NIV) says it well: "Repent, then, and turn to God, so that your sins may be wiped out, that times of refreshing may come from the Lord."

God wants our hearts. He wants us to love Him. The people in Old Testament Bible times still had to offer animal sacrifices to cover their sins. Many of them ended up doing that just because they were told to and because everyone else had to do it too—not because they loved God and were sorry for their sins. This made God sad.

It's kind of like how some kids go to church only because their parents make them. God wants you to worship Him because you want to and because you love Him, not because someone made you do it. Make sense? How can you show your love for God today?

Lord God, please forgive me for the times I don't love You very well, when my heart just isn't in it. I want to learn how to love You more.

GET RID OF SELFISHNESS

That is why the LORD says, "Turn to me now,
while there is time. Give me your hearts."
JOEL 2:12 NLT

. . . .

Can you guess what the main message of the book of Joel is? You got it! Repent and turn back to God! Why do we keep hearing this same message over and over again? Why aren't God's people getting it? God is all-powerful and loving and good. Why would anyone not want to follow Him? God is the ruler of everything. So why would anyone ever want to live without Him? Why would anyone ever disobey Him? People want control of their own lives. Kids want to do what they want and not have to obey someone else all the time. The *idea* of following God or obeying your parents sounds good, but when that video game or crafty channel on YouTube Kids is calling, it's easy to get a little selfish, right?

The prophet Joel urged people to give up their selfishness and turn back to God.

> Lord, show me any selfishness that lives in
> my heart. Please forgive me and help me
> turn to You instead of the things I want.

LET GOD HELP

Do what is good and run from evil so that you may live! Then the Lord God of Heaven's Armies will be your helper, just as you have claimed. Hate evil and love what is good; turn your courts into true halls of justice. Perhaps even yet the Lord God of Heaven's Armies will have mercy on the remnant of his people.
Amos 5:14–15 nlt

. . . .

God's people were at it again! Still plugging their ears and doing whatever they wanted. So God sent Amos, a humble shepherd. God told him to go all the way to the northern kingdom and deliver His message to Israel. Amos communicated the message boldly, telling the people of their sins and how far they'd wandered from God. But God always gives hope. He promised to forgive their sins if they returned to Him. "Seek me and live," God said (Amos 5:4 niv).

God Himself will be your helper when you turn to Him. You don't have to find strength on your own to keep following God. Let Him help.

Lord, help me to turn from all evil things and love You well. I know You will help me learn how to do that.

47

BACK OFF, BULLIES!

"Do not look down on your brother in the day of his trouble."
Obadiah 1:12 nlv

. . . .

When someone calls a human mom a "mama bear," it's because moms are known for protecting their kids from harm just like a mama bear protects her cubs. It's a fierce kind of love and protection, so watch out if you get in a mama bear's way when her kids are in danger!

That's kind of like what we see here in the book of Obadiah. Obadiah is the shortest book in the Old Testament. It's only one chapter long. It was written to the Edomites, who were relatives of the Israelites (God's children) up in the mountains. The Edomites were the bullies. They had harmed God's people, and so Obadiah delivered a message of doom to them. God punished them for what they did to His kids.

God cares so much for His children. And if you've received Jesus Christ as your Savior, you are one of God's kids too. He is just and good. You are under His protection and care.

Father God, thank You for caring about
me so much! I'm thankful You are
watching over me and protecting me.

JONAH AND THE WHALE

When God saw what they did and how they turned
from their evil ways, he relented and did not bring
on them the destruction he had threatened.
JONAH 3:10 NIV

Do you remember the story of Jonah and the whale? God told Jonah to do something he didn't want to do. So he ran away. Sometimes running away looks like keeping very busy with lots of distractions so that we don't hear from God or have to do what He says. Jonah jumped on a ship and sailed away, ignoring God's voice. His actions endangered the other men on the ship, though. So Jonah ended up in the middle of the sea because he didn't want to obey God.

Remember what happened next? A giant fish swam by and swallowed him up! Jonah spent three days inside there. Now that sure got his attention!

Jonah prayed to God, and God heard him and delivered him back to dry land. And *then* Jonah finally obeyed. He gave God's message to some evil people, and they repented and turned their hearts to God.

Lord, help me learn from Jonah's story
that I should obey You the first time!

WALKING HUMBLY WITH GOD

Do not gloat over me, my enemies! For though I fall, I will rise again. Though I sit in darkness, the LORD will be my light.
MICAH 7:8 NLT

In the Old Testament book of Micah, the people of Israel continued to disobey God. They were making really bad choices. . .even building altars to false gods! You may be tempted to think, *What is up with these people? Why do they keep forgetting God over and over?* But remember, we forget to obey God sometimes too. We need His grace and forgiveness every day.

God was still loving and patient with His children, sending messages of repentance and hope. He used a prophet named Micah to remind them of what He wanted them to do. Listen to the Lord's message in Micah 6:8 (NLV): "O man, He has told you what is good. What does the Lord ask of you but to do what is fair and to love kindness, and to walk without pride with your God?"

Lord, be my light. Please help me to walk humbly with You each day in a way that makes You smile!

GOD IS TRUSTWORTHY AND SAFE

The Lord is good, a safe place in times of trouble. And
He knows those who come to Him to be safe.
NAHUM 1:7 NLV

Nahum the prophet was sent to Nineveh just like Jonah was. But this was about one hundred years later. The Ninevites had forgotten God and turned their land back into an evil place. They did very bad things, and Nahum told them that God was going to punish them for all their wickedness.

Nahum 1:3 (NLV) says, "The Lord is slow to anger and great in power." God is patient and loving with us. And He is just. That means He is a God of justice. He's the only perfect judge who sees everything from every angle. He is the only One who knows what is truly in our hearts. He can always be trusted to do the right thing, even when we don't understand.

Lord, thank You for being my safe place. I know
I can come to You because of Jesus, who took
the full punishment for my sins. Thank You
for Your patience and love. Help me trust You
even when I don't understand Your ways.

CONFIDENT TRUST

The Lord God is my strength. He has made my feet like the
feet of a deer, and He makes me walk on high places.
HABAKKUK 3:19 NLV

• •

The prophet Habakkuk had a lot of hard questions for God. He wanted to know why people were still getting away with evil. Why so much violence? Why all the suffering? God answered him: "Look among the nations, and see! Be surprised and full of wonder! For I am doing something in your days that you would not believe if you were told" (Habakkuk 1:5 NLV).

God does things much differently than we would. In Isaiah 55:8–9 (NIV) we read, " 'For my thoughts are not your thoughts, neither are your ways my ways,' declares the LORD. 'As the heavens are higher than the earth, so are my ways higher than your ways and my thoughts than your thoughts.' "

No matter what happens, we can trust God to do the best thing. He is always trustworthy, and He is always good. Notice that the book of Habakkuk ends with a prayer of praise and confidence!

Lord, just as a deer runs confidently
through all kinds of terrain, please give me
confidence to trust You no matter what.

AMAZING LOVE

"The Lord your God is with you, a Powerful One Who wins the battle. He will have much joy over you. With His love He will give you new life. He will have joy over you with loud singing."
ZEPHANIAH 3:17 NLV

• •

The prophet Zephaniah brought a message of destruction and judgment on the disobedient children of God, but there was also hope. You know the message: *Repent and turn your hearts back to God!*

God judges all sin. He hates it. But He loves His children so very much. Because of Jesus, you don't have to be afraid of the punishment for sin. In God's great love, He made a way through Jesus for you and everyone who believes in Him to be saved and washed clean. Jesus took all our punishment for sin on the cross.

Read today's verse again. Let the message wash over you. God is with you. He delights in you. He gives you new life in Jesus. He even sings over you with joy! How amazing is that?

Jesus, You won the battle over sin.
Thank You for Your amazing love for me.

GOD WILL HELP YOU

Now this is what the Lord Almighty says:
"Give careful thought to your ways."
HAGGAI 1:5 NIV

• •

After seventy years, God's people were finally permitted to leave Babylon and go back to their homeland. Their first priority was to rebuild God's temple. They started out well, but then they got distracted by all the things they wanted for their own families. Haggai had a special message for them: *Get back to the work God gave you to do! God is with you! He will help you!*

Haggai 2:5 in *The Message* says, " 'Yes, get to work! For I am with you.' The GOD-of-the-Angel-Armies is speaking! 'Put into action the word I covenanted with you when you left Egypt. I'm living and breathing among you right now. Don't be timid. Don't hold back.' "

The God of Angel Armies is your God too. He is with you and for you. He's living and breathing in you. With His Spirit alive and at work in you, you can do anything He asks of you!

Lord, I'm so thankful Your Spirit is alive and at work
in me, helping me to do anything You ask of me.

THE HOPE OF THE WORLD

So tell them, "The Lord of All says,
'Return to Me, that I may return to you.'"
ZECHARIAH 1:3 NLV

• •

The prophet Zechariah proclaimed what all the other prophets said (say it with me now): *Repent! Turn back to God!* He encouraged the people to finish their work on the temple, but then he shared a really awesome message: Jesus, the Messiah, was coming!

Zechariah predicted in great detail things that wouldn't happen for another five hundred years. Zechariah 9:9 (NLT) says, "Rejoice, O people of Zion! Shout in triumph, O people of Jerusalem! Look, your king is coming to you. He is righteous and victorious, yet he is humble, riding on a donkey—riding on a donkey's colt."

Zechariah got to proclaim the hope of the whole world to God's people. And God kept His promise. Jesus came to take away the sin of the world (John 1:29). The humble King of the universe came to take away all of our sin and shame. He calls us out of darkness and into His wonderful light (1 Peter 2:9).

Father God, thank You for keeping Your promise
and bringing us hope in Jesus Christ.

SET YOUR HEART ON JESUS

*"But for you who fear my name, the Sun of Righteousness
will rise with healing in his wings. And you will go free,
leaping with joy like calves let out to pasture."*
MALACHI 4:2 NLT

• •

Malachi is the very last book in the Old Testament. As a prophet, Malachi delivered God's message once again. You know the one! In Malachi 2:2 (NLV), God urges the people, "Set your heart to honor My name."

As a girl who is made for more, you can set your heart to honor God's name too. As you walk with Jesus throughout your lifetime, allowing His Spirit to live and breathe through you, He teaches you everything you need to know to honor His name. You don't have to live in fear that you're getting it wrong. Jesus Himself will show you.

Read what God says in Psalm 32:8 (NIV): "I will instruct you and teach you in the way you should go; I will counsel you with my loving eye on you."

Lord, thank You for pointing me to my need
for Jesus all throughout the Old Testament.
Thank You for coming alive in me and
teaching me how to set my heart on You!

THE RESCUE PLAN

While he was thinking about this, an angel of the Lord came to him in a dream. The angel said, "Joseph, son of David, do not be afraid to take Mary as your wife. She is to become a mother by the Holy Spirit. A Son will be born to her. You will give Him the name Jesus because He will save His people from the punishment of their sins."
MATTHEW 1:20–21 NLV

• •

Hundreds of years had passed since the book of Malachi was written, and God's people continued to wait for the promised Messiah. Matthew was one of Jesus' disciples, and he wrote this book to show that Jesus Christ was, in fact, the Messiah whom the Old Testament prophets foretold.

Matthew 1:23 (ESV) says, " 'Behold, the virgin shall conceive and bear a son, and they shall call his name Immanuel' (which means, God with us)."

God's rescue plan was finally here. The world would never be the same. "The people living in darkness have seen a great light; on those living in the land of the shadow of death a light has dawned" (Matthew 4:16 NIV).

Father God, thank You for sending Jesus
and for keeping all of Your promises.

BEST FRIENDS WITH JESUS

"Ask, and what you are asking for will be given to you. Look, and what you are looking for you will find. Knock, and the door you are knocking on will be opened to you. Everyone who asks receives what he asks for. Everyone who looks finds what he is looking for. Everyone who knocks has the door opened to him."
MATTHEW 7:7–8 NLV

• •

Jesus knows everything about you. And even though He knows exactly what your heart wants and needs, He still wants you to talk to Him about those things. Jesus wants to be your Best Friend and talk to you about everything.

As you get to know more about Jesus, you'll realize how fun He is to be with. He loves to give you little surprises and blessings. He cares about you more than any other person ever could. The Bible says that He delights in you! He loves being with you and spending special time together. Ask Jesus to become your Best Friend, and you'll begin to see just how amazing His friendship can be!

Jesus, I really want to get to know You better! Will You show me how special and fun our friendship can be?

MY TEACHER, JESUS

*Then Jesus finished talking. The people were surprised
and wondered about His teaching. He was teaching
them as One Who has the right and the power to teach.
He did not teach as the teachers of the Law.*
MATTHEW 7:28–29 NLV

• •

You probably have a lot of teachers: your parents at home, as well
as leaders and teachers at church and at school. Now imagine being
taught by a teacher who created all things and knows the answer to
absolutely everything! The amazing news is that Jesus really does want
to teach you Himself! Isaiah 54:13 (NIV) says, "All your children will be
taught by the LORD, and great will be their peace."

If you've received Jesus as your Savior, His Spirit is alive in you,
teaching you all things. Jesus has complete authority and power over
all things. Why is this important for you? It means that you can go to
Jesus with all your questions. It means that He is bigger than all your
problems, failures, and fears. And you have access to this power at
every moment!

> Lord Jesus, I trust You to teach me
> everything You want me to know at just
> the right time. Help me to be listening.

COME TO JESUS

"Come to me, all you who are weary and burdened, and I will give you rest. Take my yoke upon you and learn from me, for I am gentle and humble in heart, and you will find rest for your souls. For my yoke is easy and my burden is light."
MATTHEW 11:28–30 NIV

Jesus liked to use visual imagery to help explain things to people. A yoke is a harness placed over a large animal or set of animals for the purpose of dragging something or carrying heavy equipment, often used for plowing fields long ago.

Is anything bothering you or worrying you? Do you have a problem you just don't know how to fix? Can you picture all of the burdens you are carrying right now strapped to your back? Now imagine yourself unloading each one of those burdens onto Jesus' shoulders instead. Take a deep breath. Let Jesus take away all of your worries. Yoke yourself to Him. He wants to help.

Jesus, thank You for taking my burdens. I give them fully to You. Help me not to take them back! I want the rest and peace that You are offering. Help me trust You with my whole heart.

EYES ON JESUS

Jesus said, "Come!" Peter got out of the boat and walked on the water to Jesus.
MATTHEW 14:29 NLV

• •

There Jesus was, walking on the water. Peter saw him and thought that if Jesus was with him, he could walk on the water too. So Peter got out of the boat and headed toward Jesus. But then he got distracted. He looked around and scared himself silly! And he started sinking.

When our eyes are focused on Jesus, we can do anything He calls us to do. But just like Peter, when we get distracted and scared by the waves and problems all around us, we start to sink. Peter cried out to God for help when he realized how crazy and unbelievable it seemed to step out in faith! But the Bible says that "immediately Jesus reached out his hand and caught him" (Matthew 14:31 NIV).

Jesus, sometimes I'm scared to step out in faith and do the things You ask me to. I forget to keep my eyes on You, and I look at everyone and everything else instead. Please fill me with Your power to overcome so that I can keep focused on You!

THE TORN CURTAIN

Then Jesus gave another loud cry and gave up His
spirit and died. At once the curtain in the house
of God was torn in two from top to bottom.
MATTHEW 27:50–51 NLV

When Jesus took His last breath, the curtain inside the temple in Jerusalem was miraculously torn in two from top to bottom. Imagine watching a huge heavy curtain tear like that all by itself! This curtain closing off the Holy of Holies was a big deal because only the high priest was allowed to go behind it once a year to make a sacrifice for the sins of all the people. God tore the curtain from top to bottom because He wanted people to know that Jesus had now made a way for all believers to enter the holy place to come to God. Jesus is the only sacrifice ever needed. Because of His death for us, all believers have access to God all the time.

People who hadn't believed in Jesus only moments earlier saw this miracle take place and knew that Jesus was telling the truth about Himself.

Jesus, I believe You are who You say
You are. I put all my trust in You.

OUR SPECIAL JOB

Jesus came and said to them, "All power has been given to Me in heaven and on earth. Go and make followers of all the nations. Baptize them in the name of the Father and of the Son and of the Holy Spirit."
MATTHEW 28:18–19 NLV

These famous last words of Jesus are also known as the Great Commission. This special job, or commission, was for the disciples, but it is also for us today. Jesus wants us to share His love with everyone and pass on the truth of Jesus to them. The disciples knew that the power of Jesus was real, and so they went and did as Jesus asked. They shared about Jesus, and the Gospel was made known far and wide and is still being made known to this day. Jesus promised to be with them always, and He promises the same thing to us. Jesus sent us His Holy Spirit to be alive in us always. Are you sharing your faith in Jesus? Ask Jesus for help and courage to do what He has asked.

Jesus, thank You for Your promise to be with me always. Please give me help and courage to share about You with those around me.

A DAY OF REST

"The Day of Rest was made for the good of man.
Man was not made for the Day of Rest."
MARK 2:27 NLV

. . . .

God gave us a good example to follow from the very beginning. After He created the world, He rested. He didn't have to—He chose to. God made us and knows that our bodies need rest.

Our world is fast paced, and people are constantly working or using social media. But you were made for way more than that! Jesus calls us to do things His way.

Although it's hard to go against the flow of our world and rest, Jesus says it's important for us to slow down and take time to refresh our bodies and our minds. Talk with your family and come up with a plan to limit your activities and screen time on Sunday or on a day of the week that works for your family. Then do something relaxing that brings you joy and peace instead of homework and screen time.

Jesus, help me to rest my brain and
my body so that I can be refreshed.

SUPERNATURAL PEACE

He got up and spoke sharp words to the wind. He said to the sea, "Be quiet! Be still." At once the wind stopped blowing. There were no more waves.
MARK 4:39 NLV

. . . .

Jesus and His disciples were on a boat when a big storm came. The disciples were terrified that they were going to die. But Jesus was sleeping peacefully in the middle of the storm. The disciples frantically woke Jesus up. Take a look at what happened: "And he awoke and rebuked the wind and said to the sea, 'Peace! Be still!' And the wind ceased, and there was a great calm" (Mark 4:39 ESV).

The next time you feel like things are out-of-control scary, pray the name of Jesus! "Peace, be still!" Philippians 4:7 (NIV) helps us understand this supernatural peace a bit more: "And the peace of God, which transcends all understanding, will guard your hearts and your minds in Christ Jesus."

God's peace is beyond anything we can understand.

Jesus, I feel relieved that I don't have to dig down into my feelings to find peace by myself! You are my peace! Help me trust You when I'm scared.

JESUS THE HEALER

Wherever He went, they would lay the sick people in the streets in the center of town where people gather. They begged Him that they might touch the bottom of His coat. Everyone who did was healed. This happened in the towns and in the cities and in the country where He went.
MARK 6:56 NLV

. . . .

Wherever Jesus went, crowds of people would follow. They knew Jesus had the power to heal. The crowds would lay sick people in the streets for Jesus to touch. All they wanted was to touch the bottom of His coat and they knew they would be healed. Imagine people who had been sick their whole lives desperate to be free of their illness. Imagine people who couldn't see and people who couldn't walk. They heard that Jesus had power. They didn't understand it yet, but they wanted to be well.

Jesus knew the state of their hearts and had loving compassion for them. He could've healed everyone on earth instantly, but He waited for people to come to Him. He wants us to come to Him like that too.

Jesus, thank You for Your healing power.
You are amazing, and You're alive in my heart!

GOD AT WORK

*"[Jesus] makes those who could not hear so they can hear.
He makes those who could not speak so they can speak."*
MARK 7:37 NLV

• •

Jesus can still open ears and mouths today. While He can and does heal people physically, He also heals people spiritually. Some people who have been hurt by others often blame God. Some people refuse to believe there even is a God. And some people believe God is real but that He is too busy to care about them. But the God who could make the deaf hear and the mute speak can still enable people to hear today.

As a girl who is made for more, you can let God use you to help bring people to Him who need to hear His truth. God's Spirit is still powerfully at work in our hearts and in our world. If you know people who seem far from God, pray. Pray that God would open their ears to believe that Jesus is real, and pray that they would ask Jesus to be Lord of their life.

Jesus, I trust that You still have power to heal people's hearts, minds, and bodies. I pray for my friends and family who need You. Be real to them, Lord Jesus.

YOU ARE SO IMPORTANT

*[Jesus] took the children in His arms. He put His hands
on them and prayed that good would come to them.*
MARK 10:16 NLV

. . . .

Many times throughout history, women and children weren't considered very important. In fact, they were often treated as property. This was not God's plan for women or children. You were made for so much more!

Jesus came to show another way. He loved women and children and spent lots of time with them. Jesus was upset when the disciples tried to keep children away from Him. He stood up for children and told the disciples not to prevent kids from approaching Him. He honored women and children and made them feel important. He said that "anyone who will not receive the kingdom of God like a little child will never enter it" (Mark 10:15 NIV). The faith of children is pure and strong. Jesus wants all of His children, old and young, to have faith like that!

I'm so thankful that I'm important to You, Jesus.
Your love for me is amazing! Help me to keep my
faith strong and pure. I know I'm safe with You.

A SERVANT LEADER

"Whoever wants to be a leader among you must be your servant, and whoever wants to be first among you must be the slave of everyone else. For even the Son of Man came not to be served but to serve others and to give his life as a ransom for many."
MARK 10:43–45 NLT

• •

The King of the universe didn't expect servants to take care of His every need. Jesus came to serve, not to be served. One time Jesus even washed the feet of His disciples before they ate. In Bible times, people would wear leather sandals and their feet would get very dirty, so a house servant would usually meet guests at the door and wash their feet before they entered. But Jesus showed that He was a humble servant leader and washed His disciples' feet Himself. They were astonished by the humility He showed. Peter tried to get Him to stop! The most powerful man in history was stooping to do a servant's job. But Jesus did this on purpose. He wants His followers to be humble and to serve others out of love for God.

Jesus, You are the very best leader. Please fill me with Your Spirit so I can lead like You do.

MIGHTY POWER

[Jesus] said to them, "You are to go to all the world
and preach the Good News to every person."
MARK 16:15 NLV

. . . .

When we commit our lives to Jesus, the Holy Spirit comes to live inside our hearts and works in us to carry out God's plans here on earth. Jesus wants us to tell everyone about this great power! Ephesians 1:19–20 (NLT) says, "I [Paul] also pray that you will understand the incredible greatness of God's power for us who believe him. This is the same mighty power that raised Christ from the dead and seated him in the place of honor at God's right hand in the heavenly realms." This mighty power is what is alive and working inside of you today. Isn't that amazing?

How can you share your story with others? How can you begin telling everyone about the great power and love of Jesus? Sit down with your family and brainstorm ideas to share God's love with those around you.

> Jesus, thank You for the power of Your Holy
> Spirit living inside of me. Please fill my
> heart with Your love and courage as I tell
> everyone about Your great love for them.

DOING THE IMPOSSIBLE

The man who was dead sat up and began to
talk. Then Jesus gave him to his mother.
LUKE 7:15 NLV

. . . .

A young man had died and his body was being carried through the town. He was the only son of a widow. Because the main wage earner in the family had died, the widow was probably going to have a lot of financial problems in the future. She was sad and probably scared. But what could be done? Her son was already dead. But then Jesus saw her. The Bible tells us that His heart went out to her. He had compassion and love for this widow who had lost her only son. He told her not to cry, and then He commanded the dead man to get up.

Jesus can take a completely hopeless situation and turn it around. Whenever you feel like a problem is completely impossible, reach out to Jesus. Trust that He can do the impossible and bring hope to hopeless situations.

Jesus, help me to trust that You can bring hope
to any situation. Show me how to share this
hope with my friends and family members.

LOVE YOUR NEIGHBOR

"Which of these three do you think was a neighbor to the man who was beaten by the robbers?" The man who knew the Law said, "The one who showed loving-pity on him." Then Jesus said, "Go and do the same."
LUKE 10:36–37 NLV

• •

A man was beaten and left for dead by robbers. Three people walked by the hurting man. The first two saw the man and passed by on the other side. The third man went to the wounded man and helped him. He bandaged his wounds and took him to an inn to heal, paying for his expenses. Which man acted like a good neighbor to the wounded man? The one who helped, of course.

What does this story mean to a girl who is made for more? Jesus says that anyone we come across is our neighbor. And Jesus wants us to love our neighbors as ourselves. Sometimes that is difficult—especially if you have unfriendly neighbors! But Jesus can help you love even the unlovable. Just ask!

Jesus, please help me love my neighbors in ways that bless You, even when it's hard.

BEING WITH JESUS

Jesus said to her, "Martha, Martha, you are worried and troubled about many things. Only a few things are important, even just one. Mary has chosen the good thing. It will not be taken away from her."
LUKE 10:41–42 NLV

Sometimes we get so distracted by the work we're doing *for* Jesus that we forget to take time to be *with* Jesus. That's what happened with Martha. She loved Jesus and was very happy to have Him in her home, but she got distracted by all the work that needed to be done to provide for Jesus' needs while He was in her home. Martha's sister Mary chose to sit at Jesus' feet and listen to Him, instead of doing what everyone else expected of her. Jesus said she made the best choice.

Are you easily distracted? God has special plans for you that He will help you accomplish if you're spending time with Him. Distractions can cause you to go down a path that wasn't meant for you. Ask Jesus to help you get rid of distractions so that you can have some quiet, focused time with Him every day.

Jesus, help me to make the best choice like Mary did.

PRAYING LiKE JESUS

Jesus said to [His disciples], "When you pray, say, 'Our Father in heaven, Your name is holy. May Your holy nation come. What You want done, may it be done on earth as it is in heaven. Give us the bread we need everyday. Forgive us our sins, as we forgive those who sin against us. Do not let us be tempted.' "
LUKE 11:2–4 NLV

God made you to have a relationship with Him. We get to know Him more by reading His Word and praying. Jesus gave us a great example of how to pray to God. He begins this prayer by praising God. By worshipping and praising God first, we open our hearts with gratitude and thanksgiving. When we get our eyes off ourselves and what we want God to do for us, we are happier and more content. Prayer is a two-way conversation, not a wish list we submit to heaven. Ask Jesus to help you learn how to pray and how to listen for His voice. He wants you to know Him.

> Jesus, help me to stop and listen when I pray. Help me learn to hear Your voice.

A LIGHT IN THE DARK

"The eye is the light of the body. When your eye is good, your whole body is full of light. When your eye is sinful, your whole body is full of darkness. Be careful that the light in you is not dark. If your whole body is full of light, with no dark part, then it will shine. It will be as a lamp that gives light."
LUKE 11:34–36 NLV

• •

There is a lot of darkness in this world, and the enemy wants to load up your brain with it. Darkness and evil lurk online and in the hearts of people who don't love God. But God made you for more!

When we choose to follow Jesus, He shines His light in our hearts for all to see. Just as everyone can see the one little flashlight when all the lights go out, you can be a source of light in the darkness that surrounds you every day.

Jesus, protect me from the darkness around me. Help me to make right choices when it comes to what I look at and listen to and allow in my mind. Fill me with Your light.

PLEASING GOD INSTEAD OF PEOPLE

"When they take you to the places of worship and to the courts and to the leaders of the country, do not be worried about what you should say or how to say it. The Holy Spirit will tell you what you should say at that time."
Luke 12:11–12 nlv

. . . .

Sometimes in life people will start feeling bigger and louder than God. Grown-ups and teachers and friends might all be telling you one thing, but you know in your heart that Jesus wants you to do something else. Certain people's approval of you might seem pretty important. You want your teacher or coach or friends to like you. But it's much more important to please Jesus than to please another person.

Ask Him and He will give you the strength to say the right thing at the right time and to do what He is asking you to do. If God is feeling too small to you and people seem too big, tell Jesus how you feel. Ask for His Spirit to help you.

*Jesus, sometimes I'm confused. I need
Your help to know what to say and do.
I want to please You, not other people.*

TRUSTING JESUS WITH OUR NEEDS

"Do not worry about your life, what you are going to eat. Do not worry about your body, what you are going to wear. Life is worth more than food. The body is worth more than clothes."
Luke 12:22–23 nlv

• •

Think about the birds in your neighborhood. They don't have jobs. They don't have a kitchen with a pantry to make food for their families. But God feeds them! And think of the flowers. They don't have any money to buy clothes, yet they are stunningly beautiful. God dresses them Himself. Jesus tells us that we are more valuable to God than birds and flowers. We're His favorite! So of course He is going to take care of us.

Having nice clothes or eating yummy food is fine as long as it's not our life purpose. Jesus wants our life purpose to match up with His purpose for our lives: to love God and love others. Worrying about things like food and clothes shows that we don't trust Jesus enough to take care of our needs. Talk to Him about this.

Jesus, help me to trust You with all of my needs.

JESUS IS GOD

The Word (Christ) was in the beginning. The Word was with God. The Word was God. He was with God in the beginning. He made all things. Nothing was made without Him making it. Life began by Him. His Life was the Light for men. The Light shines in the darkness. The darkness has never been able to put out the Light.
JOHN 1:1–5 NLV

• •

John was one of Jesus' twelve disciples, so he was there to see Jesus' miracles firsthand. John begins by telling us that Jesus has always existed, even before He was born as a human on earth! Can anyone else say that? Jesus was completely God and completely man. Jesus is the image of the invisible God who made the whole world (Colossians 1:15). And Colossians 2:9 (NLT) tells us, "In Christ lives all the fullness of God in a human body." When you put your trust in Jesus, you are putting your faith in the one true God who was and is and is to come (Revelation 1:8).

> Jesus, I might not be able to understand everything about You just yet, but I do put my faith and trust in You.

YOUR SPIRITUAL BIRTHDAY

*[Jesus] gave the right and the power to become
children of God to those who received Him. He gave
this to those who put their trust in His name.*
JOHN 1:12 NLV

When you receive Jesus as your Savior, you become a child of God. John 1:13 (NLV) tells us that you become "born of God." Can you believe it? When you were born as a baby, you came alive physically. When you were "born of God," you came alive spiritually. The day you received Jesus as your Savior was your spiritual birthday. It's something fun and important to celebrate! If you know when you asked Jesus into your heart, write down the day and plan a celebration. Sing some worship songs and create a feast, thanking God for who He is and everything He has done for you. If you don't know the exact day you decided to follow Jesus, ask your family to help you estimate so you have a close idea.

Jesus, I'm so thankful I gave my life
to You and became a child of God!

GOD BECAME ONE OF US

Christ became human flesh and lived among us. We saw His shining-greatness. This greatness is given only to a much-loved Son from His Father. He was full of loving-favor and truth.
JOHN 1:14 NLV

Jesus came to earth and became a man so that we could know Him completely. He came to love us and show us the truth. Philippians 2:6–8 (ICB) tells us a bit more about this: "Christ himself was like God in everything. He was equal with God. But he did not think that being equal with God was something to be held on to. He gave up his place with God and made himself nothing. He was born as a man and became like a servant. And when he was living as a man, he humbled himself and was fully obedient to God. He obeyed even when that caused his death—death on a cross." Jesus gave up His place in heaven to come and save us!

Jesus, I'm so thankful You chose to enter our world so that we can enter Yours. I know You made me for more than I could ever imagine. I put my hope in You alone.

THE GOOD NEWS

For God so loved the world that he gave his one and only Son, that whoever believes in him shall not perish but have eternal life. For God did not send his Son into the world to condemn the world, but to save the world through him.
JOHN 3:16–17 NIV

• •

John 3:16 is maybe the most well-known verse in the Bible. It's the Good News! It's also a great verse to share with people who want to know more about Jesus. Why not try memorizing it? John 3:17 is important too. Jesus didn't come to condemn us; He came to be our Savior. And when we believe and receive Christ as our Lord and Savior, we are guaranteed eternal life—a life that lasts forever. Making Jesus Lord of our lives means that we choose to let Him lead us throughout our lives. We follow His Word and His ways.

Jesus, You've offered me eternal life, and I accept this gift. I'm so grateful You've chosen me to be Your child. Please lead me in Your truth and in Your ways. Open doors for me to share Your good news.

JESUS WILL NEVER TURN YOU AWAY

*"All whom My Father has given to Me will come to Me.
I will never turn away anyone who comes to Me."*
JOHN 6:37 NLV

. . . .

Jesus will never turn you away if you're seeking Him. Not even if you've made a huge mistake. Romans 2:4 tells us that it's the kindness of God that leads us to Jesus so that we might have our sins forgiven. If you've made a mistake, the best thing you can do is to go straight to Jesus and talk to Him about it. You can do this at school, in your backyard, in your bedroom—anywhere! Jesus promises that He will not turn you away. He will not shame you or make you feel bad about who you are. He will forgive you and help you. He will tell you He loves you and show you ways that you can change.

Jesus, thank You for Your loving-kindness to
me. When I make mistakes, remind me that You
love me and that You'll never turn me away.
You are my Best Friend and my Counselor.

THE TRUTH ABOUT YOU AND GOD

"You will know the truth and the truth will make you free."
JOHN 8:32 NLV

God wants you to know the truth about who you are and who He is. He has so much to say about this in His Word, the Bible. He very much wants you to believe what He says and live like you believe it. These truths are so important that I include them every time I write a new devotional.

Ask Jesus to help you believe these words as you read them:

- I am free and clean in the blood of Christ (1 John 1:7; Galatians 5:1).
- He has rescued me from darkness and has brought me into His kingdom (Colossians 1:13).
- I am a precious child of the Father (Isaiah 43:7; John 1:12; Galatians 3:26).
- God sings over me (Zephaniah 3:17).
- I am a friend of Christ (John 15:15).
- Nothing can separate me from God's love (Romans 8:38–39).
- God knows me intimately (Psalm 139).
- God is for me, not against me (Romans 8:31).

Knowing who you are in Christ will change your whole life forever.

*Father God, thank You for telling me
the truth. I choose to believe Your truth.
Help me live my life for You.*

RIGHT NOW AND FOREVER

"The robber comes only to steal and to kill and to destroy.
I came so they might have life, a great full life."
JOHN 10:10 NLV

• •

When you invite Jesus into your heart and choose to follow Him, the kingdom of God begins at that moment in your heart. In Luke 17:20–21 (NLV), Jesus said to them, "The holy nation of God is not coming in such a way that can be seen with the eyes. It will not be said, 'See, here it is!' or, 'There it is!' For the holy nation of God is in you."

Yes, we are waiting for Jesus to return so that we can physically be with Him for eternity. And yes, there will be a day when Jesus makes all things new and destroys all evil forever. But we don't have to wait for heaven to be a part of God's kingdom. It has already begun inside your heart! This is what you were made for.

Jesus, I'm so thankful we're friends and
that I get to experience Your love and
joy right now and for all eternity!

TRUE LOVE

"This is what I tell you to do: Love each other just as I have loved you. No one can have greater love than to give his life for his friends."
JOHN 15:12–13 NLV

. . . .

Giving up your life for someone else demonstrates true, unselfish love. It's hard to imagine that kind of love. God chose to send His Son into the world to live just like us, to become our Friend, and eventually to lay down His life and die on the cross to show how much He actually loves us. This series of events was no accident. He knew the cost. Jesus knew it would hurt. He knew He would suffer. He knew He would be betrayed by some of the people closest to Him. But He went to the cross anyway so that we could be made right with God once and for all.

His love—a love that never fails or lets us down—is available to all of us who seek Him! Ask Jesus to fill you with His love. Then share it with others!

Jesus, I'm so sorry for all the pain You went through for me. I can't imagine that kind of love. But I am forever grateful for what You've done.

THE GREAT ADVENTURE

After [Jesus] had suffered much and then died, He showed Himself alive in many sure ways for forty days. He told them many things about the holy nation of God.
ACTS 1:3 NLV

• •

Not only is the Bible the inspired Word of God, but it is a reliable historical textbook. The book of Acts shows us the history of the first churches after Jesus went back to heaven. The promised Holy Spirit was given to believers and miracles were taking place, showing the great power of the Spirit of God coming alive inside of His followers.

Jesus told His followers to go and share the Good News with everyone! And as a follower of Jesus who is made for more, you are called to share the Good News too. With the Spirit of Jesus alive and at work in your heart, you are equipped to go and do everything that God made you for. Your life will be a great adventure as you follow His plans for your life. Any good adventure includes some obstacles to overcome, so it won't always be easy. But Jesus will always be in you and with you.

Jesus, thank You for this great adventure
I'm on of loving and following You.

HOLY SPIRIT POWER

"But you will receive power when the Holy Spirit comes into your life. You will tell about Me in the city of Jerusalem and over all the countries of Judea and Samaria and to the ends of the earth."
ACTS 1:8 NLV

- -

If you're living your life to follow Jesus, other people are going to wonder about you! Some people may be unkind and make fun of you for being a Christian. Their words might even make you angry. Before you answer them, ask for God's help. He is right there with you, and He sees everything that's happening. You have Holy Spirit power available to you at all times. He can help you answer with gentleness and respect (see 1 Peter 3:15), not anger or embarrassment. The reason they're making fun or asking questions is because they are looking for hope, and they want to know if yours is real.

Jesus, help me remember that everyone is
looking for hope in You. You've created all of
us that way. Help me to be gentle and show
respect to others when I share my faith in You.
Thank You that Your Spirit is alive in me.

THE SPIRIT IS ALIVE IN US

"God says, 'In the last days I will send My Spirit on all men. Then your sons and daughters will speak God's Word. Your young men will see what God has given them to see. Your old men will dream dreams.'"
ACTS 2:17 NLV

Do you remember the prophet Joel from the Old Testament? He foretold that the Holy Spirit would be sent to us many years before it actually happened. The coming of the Holy Spirit was part of God's big plan to save His people. He knew we couldn't figure out life alone. He knew we would need a Helper to teach us and lead us. So He sent His very own Spirit to live inside of us.

When we have the Spirit of Jesus alive in us, some really cool things happen: God's Word comes to life in us, we are able to understand things that we couldn't before, and we are able to discern right and wrong. The ancient theologian Augustine said, "Without the Spirit we can neither love God nor keep His commandments." The Holy Spirit helps us to do both!

Jesus, I'm so glad You sent Your Spirit to teach me and to help me follow You.

THE MISSION

"I say to you now, stay away from these men and leave them alone. If this teaching and work is from men, it will come to nothing. If it is from God, you will not be able to stop it. You may even find yourselves fighting against God."
ACTS 5:38–39 NLV

• •

A Jewish leader told the crowd to stop being mean to the first missionaries. He reminded them that if the teachings of Jesus were real, no man would be able to stop them. And if they weren't real, nothing would happen and they would eventually stop.

As you know, the teachings of Jesus *are* real, and the Gospel has been spread far and wide for close to two thousand years! No man or government has been able to stop the spread of the Gospel, even though many have tried. One historical leader tried to burn every copy of the Bible. It is a miracle from God that we know about Jesus and have His words to read today. Part of our mission as followers of Jesus today is to keep spreading this miracle.

Jesus, I'm so thankful to have Your Word. Help me to keep spreading Your truth all over the world.

UNASHAMED

For I am not ashamed of the gospel, because it is the power of God that brings salvation to everyone who believes: first to the Jew, then to the Gentile.
ROMANS 1:16 NIV

. . . .

The Jews were God's people. All that time the prophets spent asking the children of Israel to repent and turn back to God? Those were the Jews, God's chosen people. Jesus Himself was a Jew too. But Jesus didn't come to save just the Jews; He came to save all people. You are included in that rescue plan.

Read today's verse in *The Message*: "It's news I'm most proud to proclaim, this extraordinary Message of God's powerful plan to rescue everyone who trusts him, starting with Jews and then right on to everyone else!"

As a girl who is made for more, you never have to be ashamed of the Gospel. You don't have to be embarrassed or worried about sharing your faith in Jesus with others. His Spirit lives inside you, and that makes you one powerful girl!

Lord, please forgive me for the times I've been embarrassed about my faith. Give me Your power to stand up for what I believe in, unashamed.

DON'T GIVE UP

*We are glad for our troubles also. We know that
troubles help us learn not to give up.*
ROMANS 5:3 NLV

· ·

When you're going through hard times, it's easy to get discouraged. You want things to change, and you want them to change quickly! Sometimes it can be hard to keep a good attitude when you need things to change so badly. But hard times can actually be good for us if we allow God to work in them.

The Message puts it this way: "We continue to shout our praise even when we're hemmed in with troubles, because we know how troubles can develop passionate patience in us" (Romans 5:3). While it's definitely not easy to be glad for trouble, we learn to trust Jesus more in those times, and hard times teach us to be patient too. We learn not to give up. Hard times give us an opportunity to trust God's Word as we wait patiently for God to bring good out of bad.

Jesus, I know I can give You praise and
thanks even during hard times. Help
me to trust You and not give up.

ALWAYS THERE TO HELP

When we have learned not to give up, it shows we have stood the test. When we have stood the test, it gives us hope. Hope never makes us ashamed because the love of God has come into our hearts through the Holy Spirit Who was given to us.
ROMANS 5:4–5 NLV

. . . .

Jesus is our living hope, and because of Him we can have a real friendship with God. Our hope of heaven never goes away, but we can also have great hope and peace right now. We don't need to wait for heaven to know God and experience His love, joy, power, and peace. He wants to give those things to you now. . .today!

God always keeps His promises, and He promises He will be with you always. Romans 8:28 (NIV) says, "We know that in all things God works for the good of those who love him, who have been called according to his purpose."

Take a look inside your heart. Invite Jesus to look in there too. Are you filled with love, joy, power, and peace? If not, ask Jesus to help!

Father God, thank You for teaching me never
to give up. You are always there to help.

ONLY JESUS SAVES

If you say with your mouth that Jesus is Lord, and believe in your heart that God raised Him from the dead, you will be saved from the punishment of sin.
ROMANS 10:9 NLV

• •

Sometimes people call becoming a Christian "getting saved." The Bible tells us that no one gets to God the Father unless they go through Jesus Christ alone. Nothing else saves you. Working hard to be good doesn't save you. Being a truthful person doesn't save you. Being as nice as you can be doesn't save you. Going to church doesn't save you. Saying your family is Christian doesn't save you. Belonging to a Christian church doesn't save you. Being baptized doesn't save you. Only Jesus saves.

It's a heart thing. Jesus knows your heart. He knows if what you're saying with your mouth is true. He is the only One able to look inside of you and know what's really happening. And you were made for relationship with Him!

Jesus, I believe that You are the one true God. Thank You for taking away my sins and saving me.

IN GOOD TIMES AND BAD

May the God of hope fill you with all joy and peace
as you trust in him, so that you may overflow
with hope by the power of the Holy Spirit.
ROMANS 15:13 NIV

. . . .

Can you imagine watching a movie in which nothing bad or challenging ever happened? In which the main characters didn't have to overcome any problems? That would probably be a pretty boring show! Every great adventure needs to include some difficulty to overcome, right?

You're on a great adventure with Jesus. And in good times and bad, you can overflow with hope and peace because of the power of the Holy Spirit living inside you. His presence with you makes life wonderful and worth living—even during difficult times. When you commit to following Jesus, the God of all hope changes you. Pray to the God of hope and ask Him to fill you to overflowing. He will do it!

Jesus, You are the God of hope. Thank You for
giving me this wonderful life, full of adventure.
Fill me with Your joy and peace as I trust in You!

YOU'RE SOMETHING SPECIAL!

I write to God's church in the city of Corinth. I write to those who belong to Christ Jesus and to those who are set apart by Him and made holy. I write to all the Christians everywhere who call on the name of Jesus Christ. He is our Lord and their Lord also.
1 Corinthians 1:2 NLV

· ·

There is something really quite special about you! Did you know that? God says you are set apart and made holy because of what Jesus has done for you. He is always looking on you with love. Have you ever caught your parents looking at you when they thought you were asleep? Parents get a certain love-look on their faces that they have only for their children. You have a special place in God's heart too. And He is the perfect Parent. He is always looking at you with a special look of love. Even though there are several billion people in this world He made, you are still very special to Him.

Father God, I don't understand how I could possibly be special to You, but I believe it's true! Thank You for loving me.

THE MESSAGE OF THE CROSS

*The message of the cross is foolish to those who
are headed for destruction! But we who are being
saved know it is the very power of God.*
1 Corinthians 1:18 NLT

• •

Jesus came to make us right before God forever and ever. God sent Jesus to take the blame for all the sins of everyone by dying on the cross. Three days later, He rose up from the grave, conquering death and sin for all time. This is the Gospel message. It seems silly to people who don't care about God, but as a girl who is made for more, you know how powerful it is!

Jesus came to make you right with God so that when God looks at you, He sees the righteousness (the right-ness, the perfect-ness) of Jesus. You are clean and free to live life to the full, with Jesus guiding you and blessing you.

*Wow, Lord! You see me as perfect because of Jesus?
How awesome is that! Thank You for Your love
and sacrifice for me. I love You, Lord Jesus!*

YOUR BODY IS GOD'S TEMPLE

Do you not know that your body is a house of God where the Holy Spirit lives? God gave you His Holy Spirit. Now you belong to God. You do not belong to yourselves. God bought you with a great price. So honor God with your body. You belong to Him.
1 CORINTHIANS 6:19–20 NLV

When you commit your life to Christ, His Spirit miraculously comes to live inside you and you become a temple of the Holy Spirit. The secular (non-Christian) dictionary actually defines *temple* this way: "Any place or object in which God dwells, as the body of a Christian. I Cor. 6:19."

Isn't that amazing? So if your very own body is a place where God Himself dwells, doesn't that make you want to take care of it a little better? Your body matters to God. We can take care of our temples by eating right, exercising, getting enough rest, and keeping ourselves pure. Being a temple of the Holy Spirit is a big responsibility, and we can't do it without supernatural help.

Lord God, help me to take Your words seriously.
I believe I am Your temple, and I want to
make healthy choices for my body.

GOD MAKES A WAY OUT!

God is faithful. He will not allow you to be tempted more than you can take. But when you are tempted, He will make a way for you to keep from falling into sin.
1 CORINTHIANS 10:13 NLV

• •

Our enemy, Satan, is out to trip up young people in any way he can. He often aims his arrows right at your self-control, tempting you and trying to get you to do things you know are wrong. Has this happened to you before?

The Message says, "All you need to remember is that God will never let you down; he'll never let you be pushed past your limit; he'll always be there to help you come through it" (1 Corinthians 10:13). Ask Jesus to fill you up with His power to overcome all the tricks of the enemy.

Jesus always provides a way out of temptation!

Jesus, please help me to look for the escape routes You put in my path every time I'm tempted to do the wrong thing. I know You are bigger and stronger than the enemy.

WHAT IS LOVE?

Love is patient, love is kind. It does not envy, it does not boast, it is not proud. It does not dishonor others, it is not self-seeking, it is not easily angered, it keeps no record of wrongs. Love does not delight in evil but rejoices with the truth. It always protects, always trusts, always hopes, always perseveres. Love never fails.
1 CORINTHIANS 13:4–8 NIV

• •

Most people think love is a feeling of happiness, but that's not always true. Love is a choice. You can choose to love someone even when you don't feel like it. The Bible has a lot to say about true love. It lays down its life for its friends (John 15:13). It's patient and kind. It keeps no record of wrongs. It never fails. All of those things are true of God. First John 4:8 (NIV) says, "Whoever does not love does not know God, because God is love."

True love—supernatural, unfailing love—can come only from God. Thankfully, His Spirit lives in our hearts, giving us the capacity to love that way too.

Dear God, please help me to love like You do.

HE COMFORTS US

We give thanks to the God and Father of our Lord Jesus Christ. He is our Father Who shows us loving-kindness and our God Who gives us comfort. He gives us comfort in all our troubles. Then we can comfort other people who have the same troubles. We give the same kind of comfort God gives us. As we have suffered much for Christ and have shared in His pain, we also share His great comfort.
2 Corinthians 1:3–5 nlv

· ·

We aren't guaranteed a life without suffering. Jesus Himself said that this life here on earth would have trouble (John 16:33). But the amazing thing is that we can have peace and joy here because of His presence in the midst of the trouble. He helps us move forward in love toward others.

God comforts us in our pain and then gives us courage and faith to go help comfort others in the same way. As you grow up, you'll meet a lot of hurting and broken people. God can use you in their lives in helpful ways if you let Him.

*Lord, I want to help others who are hurting.
Help me comfort them the way You comfort me.*

LIKE A BUTTERFLY

*All of us, with no covering on our faces, show the
shining-greatness of the Lord as in a mirror. All the time we
are being changed to look like Him, with more and more of His
shining-greatness. This change is from the Lord Who is the Spirit.*
2 CORINTHIANS 3:18 NLV

Have you ever seen a butterfly transform from a caterpillar into a butterfly? It's amazing to watch! The caterpillar has to stop eating, hang upside down, and spin itself into a cocoon where the metamorphosis occurs before it can become a butterfly.

God transforms us kind of like that butterfly. As you get to know Jesus and allow His Spirit to begin speaking to you and leading you, you begin to transform and start looking a lot more like Jesus. Not in terms of your hair color or facial features, but rather your heart begins to look a lot more like the heart of God.

When you start following Jesus, you'll experience freedom and love and get help with your transformation process as He prepares you to fly.

Jesus, I want my heart to look like Your heart.
Thanks for the great work You're doing in me!

READY FOR ACTION

For the love of Christ puts us into action. We are sure that Christ died for everyone. So, because of that, everyone has a part in His death. Christ died for everyone so that they would live for Him. They should not live to please themselves but for Christ Who died on a cross and was raised from the dead for them.
2 Corinthians 5:14–15 nlv

. . . .

Now that you're learning how much you matter to God and how much He loves you, you can do something about it! Jesus died for you so that you would live for Him.

How do you live for Jesus? You live for Jesus by knowing who you are in Christ (God's child), loving God, and loving others. Matthew 22:36–40 (look it up!) says that loving God and loving others sums up everything God wants you to know. The amazing thing is that God Himself will help you live for Him! His Spirit will remind you who you are and show you how to love God and others.

Lord, I'm ready for action. Help me to listen for Your Spirit so that I can learn to love You and others well.

THE REAL YOU

Therefore, if anyone is in Christ, he is a new creation.
The old has passed away; behold, the new has come.
2 CORINTHIANS 5:17 ESV

God has such great plans for your life, my friend! You were made for so much more than a boring, lackluster life. He has made you into a new creation, ready to be used for His glorious purposes. A life of adventure in Christ awaits you.

Remember what God says about you: You are a new creation. The old is gone. The new has come. You are His beloved daughter. You are chosen. You are holy and dearly loved.

This is the real you. Write it down in your journal. Tape it up in your room. Repeat it out loud every morning and every evening until you start believing it. Christ is in you (Colossians 1:27). You are a temple of the Holy Spirit (1 Corinthians 6:19). You are royalty!

I'm starting to believe what You say about me,
Lord. Increase my trust in You. Help me live like
Your royal daughter, chosen and dearly loved.

WEAPONS FOR BATTLE

We do not use those things to fight with that the world uses.
We use the things God gives to fight with and they have
power. Those things God gives to fight with destroy the
strong-places of the devil. We break down every thought and
proud thing that puts itself up against the wisdom of God.
We take hold of every thought and make it obey Christ.
2 CORINTHIANS 10:4–5 NLV

• •

You're a child of God, and so the enemy knows he has already lost the fight for your soul. But he will still do everything he can to mess with your thoughts. And the way you think has everything to do with the way you live your life.

God wants your thoughts to line up with His thoughts. He wants you to learn to take every thought captive. That means that anytime you have a disturbing or prideful thought or start to worry or obsess about something, you should take it to Jesus. Ask for His truth. Get in the habit of doing this every time and it will become second nature.

Lord, You have given me weapons to win this
war. Teach me how to think Your thoughts.

RETURNS AND EXCHANGES

He answered me, "I am all you need. I give you My loving-favor. My power works best in weak people." I am happy to be weak and have troubles so I can have Christ's power in me. . . . For when I am weak, then I am strong.
2 CORINTHIANS 12:9–10 NLV

• •

Have you ever gone with a parent to exchange something at a store? Did you get a different size or something completely different? God likes to exchange things too! He's often swapping old for new, death for life, ashes for beauty, sadness for joy, despair for praise (see Isaiah 61:3). And He also exchanges our weakness for His strength.

Do you need God to exchange something for you? What do you need to bring to Him that you would like replaced with something that only He can give? Selfishness for spiritual fruit? Sadness for joy? Weakness for strength?

You can bring all of your weaknesses to Jesus and lay them at His throne. You don't even have to wait in line! Ask Him to replace your frailties with His power.

Father God, I'm so thankful You exchange my weaknesses for Your strength.

CHRIST LIVES IN ME

I have been put up on the cross to die with Christ. I no longer live. Christ lives in me. The life I now live in this body, I live by putting my trust in the Son of God. He was the One Who loved me and gave Himself for me.
GALATIANS 2:20 NLV

. . . .

You are so important to Jesus that He gave His life for you on the cross. Right here in Galatians 2:20, the Bible says that you were with Jesus on that cross. He died for your sins and then He rose from the grave, showing that He had all power in heaven and on earth, even power over death.

His Spirit is alive in you, and you get to live out His life every day. That's what you were made for! You are an instrument that God uses to do His work on earth. Whenever you feel discouraged, remember that Jesus is alive in you!

Jesus, I'm so thankful that my life has a purpose. I'm excited that You want to use me as an instrument to do Your work here on earth. Lead me and help me listen.

EQUAL IN CHRIST

There is no longer Jew or Gentile, slave or free,
male and female. For you are all one in Christ Jesus.
GALATIANS 3:28 NLT

. . . .

You are just as important to God as your pastor, your principal, or even the president! The Bible says that God doesn't play favorites. That means He doesn't think one person is more important than another person because of what they do or how much money they have. That kind of stuff doesn't matter to God. In Acts 10:34–35 (NLV) we read, "Then Peter said, 'I can see, for sure, that God does not respect one person more than another. He is pleased with any man in any nation who honors Him and does what is right.' "

We are all equal because of Jesus. A wise person said that the closer we get to Jesus, the more equal we become. That's because God's love changes our hearts to be more like His. God's door is wide open for everyone, no matter what kind of job they do or what kind of family they come from. The love of Jesus is for everyone!

Lord God, thank You that Your door is open to
everyone! You love each of us abundantly and equally.

CHOOSING LOVE

You, my brothers and sisters, were called to be free.
But do not use your freedom to indulge the flesh;
rather, serve one another humbly in love.
GALATIANS 5:13 NIV

· ·

In the beginning, God provided a world free from cruelty, sickness, evil, and sin. He gave us the gift of experiencing life on earth with only good plans for us. But even in the Garden of Eden, Adam and Eve had the ability to choose. God wants you to love Him because you choose to, not because He forces you to.

Think of it this way: Parents don't force their kids to love them, like robots. That just pushes children away in the long run. Parents want their kids to choose to love and obey them because they love and trust their parents. And those kids who do choose to love and obey will have a much smoother life because of it.

It's the same with us and God. Use your freedom for good. Use it to love.

Thank You for my freedom, Father God.
You are a good Dad. I trust Your loving
plan for me. Help me to choose love.

SPIRITUAL FRUIT

The fruit that comes from having the Holy Spirit in our lives is: love, joy, peace, not giving up, being kind, being good, having faith, being gentle, and being the boss over our own desires.
GALATIANS 5:22–23 NLV

· ·

When the Spirit of God is at work in your heart, He produces fruit. . .the spiritual kind of fruit. If you are becoming like Jesus, you will have fruit growing in your life right now. Philippians 1:11 (NLT) says, "May you always be filled with the fruit of your salvation—the righteous character produced in your life by Jesus Christ—for this will bring much glory and praise to God."

Can you see love, joy, peace, patience, kindness, goodness, faithfulness, gentleness, and self-control taking root and expanding in your heart? If you can, know that this spiritual growth brings much glory to God! If you're not sure, start talking to Jesus about it. Ask Him to clear out your heart to make room for what He wants to plant there.

Jesus, please fill me up with the fruit of Your Spirit. I want to see You at work in my life.

CHOSEN AND ADOPTED

*Let us honor and thank the God and Father of our Lord
Jesus Christ. He has already given us a taste of what
heaven is like. Even before the world was made, God
chose us for Himself because of His love. He planned that
we should be holy and without blame as He sees us.*
EPHESIANS 1:3–4 NLV

• •

Now read Ephesians 1:4–5 from *The Message*: "Long before he laid down earth's foundations, he had us in mind, had settled on us as the focus of his love, to be made whole and holy by his love. Long, long ago he decided to adopt us into his family through Jesus Christ. (What pleasure he took in planning this!)"

Being adopted is something very special. It means that adopted kids were chosen specifically by their parents. That's exactly what God has done for you too! You have a family on earth that God has given you to care for you and love you, but the big-picture story of your life is that you have been adopted by God into His family forever.

Lord God, thank You for choosing me
to be part of Your family forever!

MIGHTY RESURRECTION POWER

*The truth is the Good News. When you heard the
truth, you put your trust in Christ. Then God marked
you by giving you His Holy Spirit as a promise.*
EPHESIANS 1:13 NLV

. . . .

When you put your trust in Jesus, God marked you as His child and placed His Spirit in your heart. Now, the same power that raised Jesus up from the grave is alive inside you (Romans 8:11)! This mighty resurrection power lives in you through Christ, who fills you to overflowing with His love and power. This power gives you the ability to love and be loved—and to live and breathe and serve.

If you start to ignore God and try to do everything on your own, you'll find that you don't have enough strength to do the right thing by yourself. You need His mighty resurrection power on a daily basis.

Jesus, please forgive me for depending on my own
strength. Place a desire in my heart to come to You
for all the power I need to love You and others well.

EMBRACE YOUR GIFTS

For we are God's handiwork, created in Christ Jesus to do good works, which God prepared in advance for us to do.
EPHESIANS 2:10 NIV

• •

Knowing that God created you for more allows you to embrace your gifts and see them bloom into something you never knew existed. It truly removes the limits from what you can do. You are working in the power of Christ now. You can do anything and everything He asks you to do because He gives you the power to do it!

Talk to God about this. Ask Him to help you embrace who He made you to be. Look at the gifts and abilities He's given you. Are you a good leader? Do you have musical gifts? Are you really smart in a certain area? Ask Him to show you the next step. Thank God for these gifts! Pray that He would remove distractions and worries that are preventing Him from using you the way He wants to. Remember, you're working through His power now, not your own.

Father God, thank You for the special gifts You've given me. I commit them to You. Show me how You want me to use them for Your kingdom.

LET YOUR LIGHT SHINE

At one time you lived in darkness. Now you are living in the light that comes from the Lord. Live as children who have the light of the Lord in them.
EPHESIANS 5:8 NLV

. . . .

Jesus said, "I am the light of the world. Whoever follows me will never walk in darkness, but will have the light of life" (John 8:12 NIV). When we follow Jesus, He fills us up with His very own light. It's the light of life that makes believers shine from the inside out.

After a long, cold winter, there's nothing like walking out into the sunshine when spring comes. The sun makes us feel warm, and we actually need the vitamin D the sun provides to be healthy! Ask Jesus to fill you with His light so that others feel warm and healthy when they are around you.

God placed you right where you are for a purpose, to be a light for those around you who still can't see in the dark. To let your light shine, you have to be connected to the light source every day, constantly in touch with Him and pointing others to Him.

Lord, please help me shine Your light in the darkness.

113

STRONG IN GOD'S STRENGTH

Our fight is not with people. It is against the leaders and the powers and the spirits of darkness in this world. It is against the demon world that works in the heavens.
EPHESIANS 6:12 NLV

• •

The Bible tells us we have an enemy. He is known as the father of lies (John 8:44), the accuser who makes us feel bad about ourselves (Revelation 12:10), and the ruler of darkness (Ephesians 6:12). But here's the really important thing you need to know: because of Jesus, Satan doesn't have any power over you (Colossians 2:15)!

Even though the enemy knows he has been defeated, he's still trying his best to get into your head and discourage you so much that you won't be able to live for Jesus. That's why Jesus wants you to stay alert and put on your armor: "Be strong with the Lord's strength. Put on the things God gives you to fight with. Then you will not fall into the traps of the devil" (Ephesians 6:10–11 NLV).

Lord, thank You for giving me armor to protect myself against the enemy. I will be strong in Your strength.

HE FINISHES WHAT HE BEGINS

*I am sure that God Who began the good work in you will keep
on working in you until the day Jesus Christ comes again.*
PHILIPPIANS 1:6 NLV

. . . .

You were put on this earth for a purpose. You were made for more.
You didn't happen by accident, and the Bible tells us that God knows
the number of your days and the number of hairs on your head. Yes,
you were brought into this world by your parents, but God is the One
who determines your purpose.

Psalm 138:8 (NLV) says, "The Lord will finish the work He started
for me. O Lord, Your loving-kindness lasts forever. Do not turn away
from the works of Your hands."

God started a good work in you the day you were born. He has
great plans for your life (Jeremiah 29:11–13) and wants to be with you
every step of the way. Seek Him for every decision, big or small. He
wants to walk with you through them all.

Father God, thanks for creating me! I'm so glad
You know everything about me and want to help me
with all my decisions. Fill me with Your Holy Spirit
and guide me closer and closer to Your heart.

LET LOVE GROW

And this is my prayer: I pray that your love will grow more and more. I pray that you will have better understanding and be wise in all things. . . . And I pray that you will be filled with the fruits of right living. These come from Jesus Christ, with honor and thanks to God.
PHILIPPIANS 1:9, 11 NLV

• •

Have you seen a garden that is overgrown with weeds? The weeds take over and hog all of the water and nutrients that the good plants need to grow. The good plants end up dying or producing very little fruit.

Selfishness can be a weed in the garden of your heart. If you plant selfishness, it can take over and harm the good fruits of the Spirit that God has planted in your heart. Selfishness can choke out love and keep it from growing.

Don't forget, though, that Jesus is a really good gardener! He knows what to do with all the weeds. If you have weeds of selfishness growing, ask Jesus for help. He can get rid of all the weeds and help you grow love and other kinds of healthy fruit instead.

Jesus, please remove any weeds that are growing in my heart. Let love and good fruit grow instead.

THE POWER OF JESUS' NAME

*So when the name of Jesus is spoken, everyone in heaven and
on earth and under the earth will bow down before Him.*
PHILIPPIANS 2:10 NLV

• •

How do you end your prayers? By saying, "Amen," or "In Jesus' name
I pray"?

The Bible tells us that the name of Jesus is very powerful. That's
why many Christians end their prayers with "In Jesus' name."

Some of the most powerful prayers are simply "Jesus!" In those
quick moments when that is all you can think to pray, you are putting
your trust in the power of Jesus and asking for His help and protection.

Saying the name of Jesus is not some magical act that will have
power on its own. People use the name of Jesus all the time without
even a thought toward Him. (The Bible calls that taking God's name
in vain.) When you call on Jesus' name in prayer, you are showing your
hope and trust in Jesus Himself, who holds all the power. You can call
on the name of Jesus for help in any and every situation.

*Jesus, I trust that Your power is unlimited.
Please come to my rescue.*

PEACE THAT DOESN'T MAKE SENSE

Don't worry about anything; instead, pray about everything. Tell God what you need, and thank him for all he has done. Then you will experience God's peace, which exceeds anything we can understand. His peace will guard your hearts and minds as you live in Christ Jesus.
PHILIPPIANS 4:6–7 NLT

. . . .

When you hold worry inside of you, science and life experience have proven it can cause great harm to your body. Carrying heavy burdens inside of you is a dangerous thing, especially during times of change. Have you ever been scared to go to a new class or move to a new home?

God wants you to bring your fears and worries to Him instead. He promises that when you do, a very powerful thing happens: He gives you His peace. It's a peace that doesn't really make sense to anyone else but you and God, and He gives it to you no matter what you're facing. He wants you to be thankful instead of stressed, and He alone can help you do that.

Jesus, I'm feeling scared. Would You please give me Your peace that doesn't make sense? I need You. Please help.

CHECK YOUR THOUGHTS

Keep your minds thinking about whatever is true, whatever is respected, whatever is right, whatever is pure, whatever can be loved, and whatever is well thought of. If there is anything good and worth giving thanks for, think about these things.
PHILIPPIANS 4:8 NLV

Sometimes our thoughts can get us in trouble. James 1:14–15 (NLT) shows us how this works: "Temptation comes from our own desires, which entice us and drag us away. These desires give birth to sinful actions. And when sin is allowed to grow, it gives birth to death."

A simple thought, left unchecked, can lead you down a dark road. Have you experienced this? You think about something you know is wrong. You think about it some more. And eventually you go and do it.

So how do we prevent that from happening? To stay pure in our thoughts, we have to learn to take every thought captive and make it obedient to Christ (2 Corinthians 10:5). We can do that only with God's help. Ask Jesus to step right into your thoughts and change them!

Jesus, Your name is power. I pray You will step in and change my thoughts to be pure and true!

MY DAILY WALK WITH GOD

I ask God that you may know what He wants you to do. I ask God to fill you with the wisdom and understanding the Holy Spirit gives. Then your lives will please the Lord. You will do every kind of good work, and you will know more about God. I pray that God's great power will make you strong, and that you will have joy as you wait and do not give up. I pray that you will be giving thanks to the Father. He has made it so you could share the good things given to those who belong to Christ who are in the light. God took us out of a life of darkness. He has put us in the holy nation of His much-loved Son. We have been bought by His blood and made free. Our sins are forgiven through Him.
COLOSSIANS 1:9–14 NLV

- -

Today's scripture is really long. But it is a prayer for you and a great summary of what the daily Christian life looks like. Read it again. What does Jesus want you to know about this?

Jesus, I know You made me for more. Thank You for the power and strength to live my daily life for You.

MORE ABOUT JESUS

Christ is as God is. God cannot be seen. Christ lived before anything was made. Christ made everything in the heavens and on the earth. He made everything that is seen and things that are not seen. He made all the powers of heaven. Everything was made by Him and for Him.
COLOSSIANS 1:15–16 NLV

The book of Colossians tells us some really important things about Jesus Christ. As a girl who is made for more, you need to know who you are following and why. Here are some other important things to know and remember about Jesus:

- Jesus came so that we could know God (John 1:18).
- Jesus came to save us from our sins so we can live forever (John 3:16–17).
- Jesus is God in human form (Colossians 1:15).
- Jesus is the only way to God (John 14:6).
- Jesus loves you (John 15:9)!

Whenever you have a question about Jesus or you're confused about something, just ask Him! Matthew 11:25 (NIV) tells us: "At that time Jesus said, 'I praise you, Father, Lord of heaven and earth, because you have hidden these things from the wise and learned, and revealed them to little children.' "

Jesus, I'm thankful that You want to
teach me more about Yourself.

JESUS IN THE HARD THINGS

Since, then, you have been raised with Christ, set your hearts on things above, where Christ is seated at the right hand of God. Set your minds on things above, not on earthly things.
COLOSSIANS 3:1–2 NIV

• •

Have you ever gone through a really hard season in life when a bunch of problems seemed to come at you all at once? One time my daughter Jessa had a broken leg, and then she got sick with the flu and ended up missing all her favorite sports and get-togethers for nearly four months! That was a really hard time for a ten-year-old girl!

God wants to bless us in the midst of the hard things of life. He asks us to take our eyes off the hard things here on earth and look to Him instead. Daily He sends little reminders and special encouragement that He is with us and watching over us.

Thank You, Lord, for all of the simple blessings that I have in my life right now. Help me to be thankful even during hard times. Help me know You're with me. Encourage my heart and help me look to You.

SEE YOURSELF AS GOD SEES YOU

*Therefore, as God's chosen people, holy and
dearly loved, clothe yourselves with compassion,
kindness, humility, gentleness and patience.*
COLOSSIANS 3:12 NIV

You are God's chosen girl. Made for more. Holy and dearly loved. Write that down. Pin it to your bulletin board or tape it on your mirror. Ask God to help you see yourself as He sees you. This frees you up to live a life of purpose and to move forward in love. Believing God's truth about you allows you to let go of wrong thinking or any lies you might be believing about yourself.

You are God's masterpiece (Ephesians 2:10). You are made perfect in Christ (Hebrews 10:14). You have been chosen by God to bring Him glory. God says so, and all His words are truth! Look it up! Memorize it. Write it down and put it everywhere to help you remember.

Ask God for help in believing the truth about yourself. He wants you to know who you really are.

*Father God, I need a lot of help to see myself as You
see me. Speak the truth to me. Help me believe it.*

EVERYTHING YOU DO MATTERS

Whatever work you do, do it with all your heart. Do it for the Lord and not for men. Remember that you will get your reward from the Lord. He will give you what you should receive. You are working for the Lord Christ.
COLOSSIANS 3:23–24 NLV

No matter what you're working on, it can be an act of worship to God. God sees you as you clean your room and do your chores at home. Everything you do matters to God. When you realize you're actually serving and worshipping God as you work, you become a joy to your parents too. Ask God to help you with your chores and your homework. Pray for Him to give you joy in serving and helping around the house. Turning on some worship music while you work always helps too!

Lord, please help me work willingly at whatever I do, and remind me that it's all about You and for You anyway! Help me to work hard at the tasks You've given me and to do the ones I don't enjoy with a good attitude.

RUNNING FROM GOD

We know, dear brothers and sisters, that God loves
you and has chosen you to be his own people.
1 THESSALONIANS 1:4 NLT

· ·

Have you ever tried to run and hide from God? Maybe you knew He wanted you to do something, but you really, really didn't want to do it. Remember when we talked about Jonah doing that? The thing is you can run away from God, but you can never hide from Him. He has chosen you and He sees you always (see Jeremiah 23:23–24).

John 15:16 (NIV) says, "You did not choose me, but I chose you and appointed you so that you might go and bear fruit—fruit that will last—and so that whatever you ask in my name the Father will give you."

You've been chosen by God to bear fruit. The more you run, the more exhausted you become. Come back to Jesus and find the rest your soul needs. You are safe in His care. He has good plans for you.

Lord, I'm sorry for the times I've run away from You.
Help me trust Your good plans for me, and please give
me Your courage and strength to do what You ask.

GROW LIKE A HEALTHY TREE

We always thank God that when you heard the Word of God from us, you believed it. You did not receive it as from men, but you received it as the Word of God. That is what it is. It is at work in the lives of you who believe.
1 Thessalonians 2:13 nlv

When we allow the Word of God to be a daily blessing in our lives, it helps us grow like healthy trees planted along the riverbank.

Look at this passage of scripture: "They delight in the law of the Lord, meditating on it day and night. They are like trees planted along the riverbank, bearing fruit each season. Their leaves never wither, and they prosper in all they do" (Psalm 1:2–3 nlt).

Through the Holy Spirit, we have the very source of life itself alive and at work in us! So you can stop striving to make things work out on your own and rest in the fact that Jesus Himself will help you grow, prosper, and mature as you follow Him.

Lord, please give me a deep love for Your
Word. I want to grow like a healthy tree.
Thanks for doing all that work in me.

HOLINESS

For God has not called us to live in sin. He has called us to live a holy life.
1 Thessalonians 4:7 nlv

. . . .

Let's talk about holiness today. What does that even mean? First Corinthians 1:30 (NLT) tells us that "Christ made us right with God; he made us pure and holy, and he freed us from sin." Righteousness means being right with God. Because of Jesus, nothing can change the fact that God sees us as pure and holy, clean before God. Jesus took the full punishment for our mistakes. We are not held eternally responsible for sin. So that means we are right with God, or righteous.

When you remind yourself of this truth every day, you are protecting your heart from lies and discouragement. You don't have to work hard to take your sins away. That battle has been won by Jesus. He alone provides the will and the way to be holy.

Jesus, thank You for taking the punishment for all of my sin and making me holy and righteous before God. Please protect my heart from sin and discouragement.

ENCOURAGING OTHERS

*So comfort each other and make each other
strong as you are already doing.*
1 THESSALONIANS 5:11 NLV

• •

The New International Version says it this way: "Therefore encourage one another and build each other up, just as in fact you are doing."

Your relationships matter to Jesus. He made you to be in community with other people. We learn from each other and grow and share God's love when we live in relationship with other people. God doesn't want us to be lonely. You are a child of God, so that means you are part of God's family! Christians all over the world are your brothers and sisters in Christ. Being part of the family of God means that you have a responsibility to share with your fellow believers and encourage them.

If you're having a hard time finding good friends right now, ask Jesus for help! He cares about your relationships and wants you to have the family of God around you to help you in this life.

> Jesus, please help me connect with other
> believers who love You and want to follow
> You. Help me to be encouraged by them
> and help me to encourage others too.

GOD'S WILL FOR YOU

Be full of joy all the time. Never stop praying. In everything give thanks. This is what God wants you to do because of Christ Jesus.
1 Thessalonians 5:16–18 nlv

You've heard people talk about "God's will" before, right? Sometimes God's will is very clear, like it is here in 1 Thessalonians. God clearly indicates what He wants you to do: Be joyful. Pray always. Give thanks in everything. Those are three very clear statements of God's will for you.

You might look at this passage and think, *How can I possibly be full of joy all the time? How can I never stop praying? How can I be thankful all the time?* Well, the Bible answers those questions too. You can't do it on your own. You can do what God wants you to do only by the power of Jesus working in you.

When you follow Jesus and commit to doing His will, you'll begin to see joy and thankfulness bubbling up inside you as you become more and more like Him.

I commit to following You, Jesus. Thank You for being clear with me about Your will for my life. I'm so thankful I have Your power at work inside me to help me carry out Your purposes.

HONORING GOD BY BEING YOU

In this way, the name of the Lord Jesus Christ will be honored by you and you will be honored by Him. It is through the loving-favor of our God and of the Lord Jesus Christ.
2 THESSALONIANS 1:12 NLV

. . . .

Want to know the best way to share the love of Jesus with others? Be you! Simply be the amazing person God created you to be! Matthew 5:16 (NIV) says, "Let your light shine before others, that they may see your good deeds and glorify your Father in heaven."

God gave each of us special gifts to use to glorify Him and show others how amazing He is! Not sure what gifts you have? Ask Jesus to show you the special gifts and talents He put inside of you. Ask your parents or other trusted grown-ups what makes you special. A lot of times, other people can see what's special about us better than we can.

Jesus, please open my eyes and heart to see the ways You have made me special. Help me to be brave as I use these special gifts to honor You.

YOU ARE HIS

Our Lord Jesus Christ and God our Father loves us. Through His loving-favor He gives us comfort and hope that lasts forever.
2 Thessalonians 2:16 nlv

. . . .

Have you ever felt like you don't fit in or don't belong? It's important that you know that you belong to God. He wants you to know that no matter where you are, you are His! He knows your name, He is with you, and you never have to be afraid in new places or situations.

Isaiah 43:1 (nlv) says, "But now the Lord Who made you, O Jacob, and He Who made you, O Israel, says, 'Do not be afraid. For I have bought you and made you free. I have called you by name. You are Mine!' "

When Jesus Himself tells you who you are, it changes everything. You are His beloved child. He paid the price for your freedom when He gave His life for you on the cross. You have direct access to the One who sees everything and knows everything. You can be confident in every situation.

Thank You for making me Your child, Lord.
I'm so thankful I'm never alone.

THE PEACE OF JESUS

May the Lord of peace give you His peace
at all times. The Lord be with you all.
2 THESSALONIANS 3:16 NLV

. . . .

The amazing adventure God made you for is accompanied by the peace that only Jesus can give. Jesus said, "Peace I leave with you. My peace I give to you. I do not give peace to you as the world gives. Do not let your hearts be troubled or afraid" (John 14:27 NLV).

What does peace mean actually? When people who don't know Jesus talk about peace, it usually means they want quiet and a time of no problems. But Jesus wasn't talking about the kind of peace the world wants. It has been said that God's peace isn't the absence of trouble but the presence of God in the midst of trouble.

Peace is about the presence of God, no matter what kind of situation you face, good or bad. It's trusting that God has the very best planned for you, even if bad things happen.

Thank You that I don't have to be
afraid even when bad things happen.
Fill me with Your peace, Lord Jesus.

REAL-LIFE FAITH

We want to see our teaching help you have a true love that comes from a pure heart. Such love comes from a heart that says we are not guilty and from a faith that does not pretend.
1 TIMOTHY 1:5 NLV

A young missionary named Timothy was spreading God's Word. Paul, one of Jesus' followers, was teaching him. He said, "The purpose of my instruction is that all believers would be filled with love that comes from a pure heart, a clear conscience, and genuine faith" (1 Timothy 1:5 NLT).

Paul said his purpose in teaching Timothy was that believers would have a true love springing from a pure heart, a clear conscience, and real-life faith. And Jesus Himself told us that loving God and loving others is all that really matters.

The Christian life is all about love from a pure heart. When it becomes more about rules and religion, that is not real or genuine faith in Jesus. Ask God to fill your heart with His pure love and to make your faith come alive.

Jesus, please guard my heart as I grow up. Fill me with Your loving presence and make my faith real.

THE WORST OF SINNERS

What I say is true and all the world should receive it.
Christ Jesus came into the world to save sinners from
their sin and I am the worst sinner. And yet God had
loving-kindness for me. Jesus Christ used me to show how
long He will wait for even the worst sinners. In that way,
others will know they can have life that lasts forever also.
1 TIMOTHY 1:15–16 NLV

Do you know the story of the apostle Paul? He was a religious leader, or Pharisee, who did bad things to Christians. He even looked on in approval as Stephen, one of Jesus' followers, was stoned to death! But then Paul met Jesus. And it changed the whole world.

Paul called himself "the worst of sinners" because he remembered what he used to be. But God completely forgave him, transforming his heart and his life. God used Paul to further His kingdom throughout the entire world.

Lord, I know if You can use Paul, You can use me!
Thank You for cleaning up my heart and making
me for more than I ever dreamed was possible.

JUST BE YOU

Everything God made is good. We should not put anything aside if we can take it and thank God for it.
1 TIMOTHY 4:4 NLV

• •

God created you, and everything He created is good! So be the person God created you to be. You might wish you were more outgoing like some of your friends or that you looked a little different. . .but God created you exactly the way He wanted you to be.

Your personality is part of the way God made you, and He wants to use it for His glory. He also gave you the body you have for a reason, so take good care of it and thank Him for it. Ask God to change your heart to match His desires for you.

God looks at you and sees a work of art. Ask Him to give you that same attitude about yourself—not so you'll be prideful or full of yourself, but so you will respect and enjoy the body and personality God gave you!

Lord God, please change my heart to match Yours.
Help me to believe that what You say is true. Help
me to be myself—just the way You made me.

YOU'RE IMPORTANT

Let no one show little respect for you because you are young.
Show other Christians how to live by your life. They should
be able to follow you in the way you talk and in what you do.
Show them how to live in faith and in love and in holy living.
1 TIMOTHY 4:12 NLV

. . . .

You are very important to God. The New International Version puts 1 Timothy 4:12 this way: "Don't let anyone look down on you because you are young."

Jesus has always loved children and has a special respect for them. Remember, the Spirit of God is alive in you! The same Spirit lives in each one of us, from children who've recently accepted Christ to believers who've walked with Christ for a lifetime.

Christ in you makes all the difference! He gives you the power to be an example to others. As a young girl, you can inspire and encourage anyone God puts in your life, no matter how old or young they are.

Father God, thank You for reminding me that
I'm important. Please help me to be a good
example to everyone around me, young and old.

A GENEROUS HEART

*Tell those rich in this world's wealth to quit being so full of
themselves and so obsessed with money, which is here today and
gone tomorrow. Tell them to go after God, who piles on all the
riches we could ever manage—to do good, to be rich in helping
others, to be extravagantly generous. If they do that, they'll
build a treasury that will last, gaining life that is truly life.*
1 TIMOTHY 6:18–19 MSG

Today's verses really tell it like it is! Having a lot of money and getting
more money is the number one priority on many people's list. What
about yours? Do you find yourself wishing you had more money? Do
you keep wishing for more and more stuff? Ask God to change your
desires to match His. Ask Him to make you extra generous with what
you already have and to cultivate a giving heart within you. God wants
us to run after Him, not money and things that don't last.

Lord God, forgive me for the times I can only
think about getting more. I know You made me
for more than that! Help me to be content with
what I have and to develop a generous heart.

MY PERSONALITY IS FROM GOD

*For God did not give us a spirit of fear. He gave us a
spirit of power and of love and of a good mind.*
2 TIMOTHY 1:7 NLV

. . . .

God has given each of us different personalities, and nothing is wrong with the way God made you! Some of us are outgoing, some of us are curious and love school, some are creative, and some are organized and neat. However He made you, He wants you to use that personality to honor Him.

And while some of us might not like getting up in front of people, we never ever have to be afraid of what other people might say or think about us. Only God's opinion of us really matters. And He has given us His Spirit, who lives inside of us. And His Spirit is a Spirit of power, love, and self-control.

If you are ever feeling extra shy about anything, remember whose Spirit you can depend on. Ask Him to show up in big ways. He always does!

Father God, thank You for my personality. You
designed me to think and act a special way. Help
me to honor You with my thoughts and actions.

READY FOR USE

If a man lives a clean life, he will be like a dish made of gold. He will be respected and set apart for good use by the owner of the house.
2 TIMOTHY 2:21 NLV

• •

If you're getting ready to eat your morning cereal, you pull a spoon out of the silverware drawer and expect it to be clean, right? It's ready for you to use it to fill your body with breakfast. This verse in 2 Timothy is kind of the same thing. If you're clean before God, you're ready for Him to use you!

He wants to use all of us to do great things, but only those who live clean lives are ready to be used for God's special purposes. If you found a dirty spoon in the silverware drawer, would you still use it to eat your cereal? Ew, gross! Nope, you'd put it right back in the dishwasher and look for a clean spoon, right? Ask God to help you stay pure so that He can use you in the very best ways.

Lord God, please give me a clean heart. Help me to live a clean life so that You can use me.

FINDING TRUE JOY

Turn away from the sinful things young people want to do. Go after what is right. Have a desire for faith and love and peace. Do this with those who pray to God from a clean heart.
2 TIMOTHY 2:22 NLV

. . . .

It's easy for kids to get obsessed with things like screen time, the best games, money, clothes, and a lot of other things that don't really matter. Some kids think they'll only be happy if they have the next best thing. But you were made for so much more than all that! And here's the truth: Obsessing over "things" will never fill you up and make you truly happy. Only God can do that.

Did you know there is a God-shaped hole inside of you that only He can fill? It's like a puzzle piece: He's the only One who can fit in that "joy" spot you have inside of you. So ask God for help to turn away from the wrong stuff and to go after His plan for your life. It's the only way to find true joy.

Father God, please forgive me for being obsessed with the wrong things. Fill me with true joy as I get to know You more.

GOD'S WORD IS A SWORD

All Scripture is God-breathed and is useful for teaching,
rebuking, correcting and training in righteousness, so that the
servant of God may be thoroughly equipped for every good work.
2 TIMOTHY 3:16–17 NIV

Ephesians 6:17 tells us about the "sword of the Spirit." The sword of the Spirit is your weapon to attack the enemy and defend yourself against attack. The sword of the Spirit is God's Word.

A soldier without a sword isn't going to be able to do very much to win the battle. You need truth from God's Word to effectively defeat the enemy. It's a vitally important part of your spiritual equipment. In fact, it's how Jesus Himself defeated Satan in Matthew 4:1–11.

Picture yourself holding your sword (God's Word!). Ask God to help you understand and remember His words so you can use them well against your enemy.

Thank You, Lord, for giving me Your armor of
protection and equipping me for everything You
have planned for me. Please show me how to use
this armor well and to know Your Word so I can
be ready when I'm attacked by the enemy.

A DAILY CHOICE

This truth also gives hope of life that lasts forever.
God promised this before the world began. He cannot lie.
TITUS 1:2 NLV

· ·

Life with Jesus is the most amazing adventure you can ever go on. And you'll have the opportunity every day of your life either to choose Jesus or to live life in your own strength. Deuteronomy 30:19–20 (NIV) says, "This day I [Moses] call the heavens and the earth as witnesses against you that I have set before you life and death, blessings and curses. Now choose life, so that you and your children may live and that you may love the LORD your God, listen to his voice, and hold fast to him. For the LORD is your life."

Here's your daily choice: To follow Jesus and stay close to Him. Or not. Choosing Jesus won't always be easy. Some days it will be downright hard. But this is the adventure you were made for. And it is always worth it. What will you choose?

Thank You for giving me life, Jesus. Help me
stay close to You all the days of my life.

BEING KIND AND GENTLE

They must not speak bad of anyone, and they must not argue. They should be gentle and kind to all people.
TITUS 3:2 NLV

The Bible talks quite a bit about being gentle. It's something we often overlook in today's world. Even in the church, people get extra busy and distracted, and gentleness isn't a focus. Often we say whatever we feel like saying even when it might hurt somebody else's feelings.

But God doesn't want us to live this way. He wants us to be gentle with each other. Just as new parents are gentle with their newborn baby, we need to be gentle in our words and actions toward others. If you have something important to say, say it! But say it with gentleness and love in your heart.

We talk a lot about being "real" or "authentic" today. But that doesn't give us an excuse to blurt out whatever we feel like saying without caring about other people's feelings. Take all your words and actions to God first, and He will help you respond in gentleness and love.

Lord God, I want to be real with You
and others, but please help me to do it
gently and with love in my heart.

WELCOMING OTHERS

*So if you consider me your partner, welcome
him as you would welcome me.*
PHILEMON 1:17 NLT

• •

Have you ever walked into a room and instantly felt like you didn't belong? That can happen in different groups and social settings, but it shouldn't happen around other believers in Jesus. Why? Because you belong with them. And you belong because God says you do.

As believers in Jesus Christ, we are all part of one body—the body of Christ. First Corinthians 12:14–15 (MSG) says, "I want you to think about how all this makes you more significant, not less. A body isn't just a single part blown up into something huge. It's all the different-but-similar parts arranged and functioning together."

As believers in Christ, we all need each other to move and grow. The next time you feel intimidated or unwelcome with other believers or at church, ask Jesus to give you courage and show you your purpose there. If you're feeling unwelcome, maybe it's because God wants you to help welcome others!

Lord, thanks for giving me a place in Your body. Help
me welcome others so they feel like they belong too.

HEARING FROM JESUS

Long ago God spoke to our early fathers in many different ways. He spoke through the early preachers. But in these last days He has spoken to us through His Son. God gave His Son everything. It was by His Son that God made the world.
HEBREWS 1:1–2 NLV

• •

Through Jesus, God created and saved the world. Jesus is God with us, God in the flesh. When you look at Jesus, you get a clear picture of God. And He can speak directly to you. When you pray, make it a conversation where you talk a little and then listen a little.

You may not hear an out-loud voice, but Jesus can speak to your heart as He answers your prayers and gives you insight. And He will make Himself clear to you if you seek Him. In Jeremiah 29:13 (NIV) God says, "You will seek me and find me when you seek me with all your heart."

Ask Jesus to speak clearly to you today. What is He saying?

Jesus, thanks for wanting to talk to me! Help me to be able to hear from You and get to know Your voice.

GOD'S WORD IS ALIVE

God's Word is living and powerful. It is sharper than a sword that cuts both ways. It cuts straight into where the soul and spirit meet and it divides them. It cuts into the joints and bones. It tells what the heart is thinking about and what it wants to do.
HEBREWS 4:12 NLV

• •

The Bible that you have in your home is an amazing tool from God. Inside, it holds wonders, mysteries, miracles, adventures. . .and it's all true! But here is the most amazing thing: it is *alive*! Did you know that? God's Word is alive. Do you know of any other book like that?

God's Word is how we get to know the truth about who God is and what He has done. It's how we begin to hear God's voice. The Holy Spirit uses words from the Bible to teach us God's will. And when you hide God's Word in your heart by reading it and memorizing it, you learn how to live a full and God-honoring life.

Father God, I thank You so much for Your
miraculous Word. Please plant a deep
love for Your Word in my heart.

ACCESS TO EVERYTHING

*Let us then approach God's throne of grace with
confidence, so that we may receive mercy and
find grace to help us in our time of need.*
HEBREWS 4:16 NIV

• •

Did you know that you have access to God's peace, joy, and presence right now while you live on earth? You don't have to wait for heaven for those things! The Holy Spirit alive inside of you will show you the way.

Psalm 16:11 (NIV) says, "You make known to me the path of life; you will fill me with joy in your presence, with eternal pleasures at your right hand."

Today's verse in Hebrews tells you that you can walk right up to God and He will fill you with peace and joy in His presence. Isn't that amazing?

Joy is much different than happiness. You can have supernatural joy even when you're sad about something. Joy is a firm hope that good is coming because of Jesus (check out Romans 15:13!).

Lord God, I ask that You would fill me with joy in Your
presence. I'm so glad I can come into Your presence
confidently. Thanks for giving me everything I need.

JESUS IS YOUR SAFE PLACE

*This hope is a safe anchor for our souls. It will
never move. This hope goes into the Holiest
Place of All behind the curtain of heaven.*
HEBREWS 6:19 NLV

• •

Sometimes the bad things that happen in this world make us feel really discouraged. Our soul needs an anchor so that we don't get tossed back and forth by our feelings.

Colossians 3:3–4 (NLV) says, "You are dead to the things of this world. Your new life is now hidden in God through Christ. Christ is our life. When He comes again, you will also be with Him to share His shining-greatness."

Thankfully, when things feel scary or hard, you can run to Jesus for safety. He is the only One who completely understands you. You are safe and secure in Him.

Bring those heavy emotions to Jesus and know that you are covered, secure, made new, and completely safe in Christ. Now and forever. Lift your head. Pray for your friends. Move forward in faith and confidence.

*Jesus, You are my life. You cover me and
make me new. You give me confidence to live
this life because You're always with me.*

MY EVER-PRESENT HELP

*And so Jesus is able, now and forever, to save from
the punishment of sin all who come to God through
Him because He lives forever to pray for them.*
HEBREWS 7:25 NLV

. . . .

Self-confidence runs out eventually. Life gets tough and even the most courageous of us get knocked down, with little left to give it another go. But that's the very place where we find that our courage was never our own anyway. Our courage comes from Christ alone. He is our ever-present help. We can hide away in Him. He prays for us! And He gives us the supernatural help we need to get back up again.

Psalm 46:1 (NIV) says, "God is our refuge and strength, an ever-present help in trouble."

Do you remember Elijah from the Old Testament? He was so done with life that he asked God to let him die. But God sent an angel to feed and minister to him instead. God can do the very same for you.

*Jesus, I'm so thankful that You are my ever-present
help. Please send the encouragement I need.*

WHAT IS FAITH?

Now faith is being sure we will get what we hope
for. It is being sure of what we cannot see.
HEBREWS 11:1 NLV

. . . .

There was a dad in the Bible who needed help with his son. His boy had struggled with a major problem since he was born. The disciples tried to help but couldn't do anything, so the dad took the boy to Jesus. This dad had some doubts. He wanted to believe Jesus could do anything, but he wasn't quite sure yet. The dad said to Jesus, "I do believe; help me overcome my unbelief!" (Mark 9:24 NIV).

Did Jesus heal the boy and increase the dad's faith? Yep!

Faith is believing in the unseen. It's trusting that God is real and that He is alive and working in our lives. Sometimes kids have a much easier time trusting God than adults do. Why do you think that is? Talk about this with your parents.

Lord God, I want my faith in You to be strong.
Forgive me for the times I've believed that I
have to do things all by myself. Please help me
overcome my unbelief and increase my faith.

THE RACE OF LIFE

All these many people who have had faith in God are around us like a cloud. Let us put every thing out of our lives that keeps us from doing what we should. Let us keep running in the race that God has planned for us.
HEBREWS 12:1 NLV

- -

When you choose to follow Jesus, He comes right alongside you the entire way. You don't have to figure things out on your own.

Imagine you're in a relay race, and Jesus hands off the baton to you. Does He then leave you to run the rest of the race by yourself? No! Instead of a relay race, our life with Jesus is more like a three-legged race. Have you ever seen one of those? Your leg is tied to a friend's leg and your arms form a side hug. You have to run and walk in sync with each other. That's what life with Jesus looks like. He is by your side, always. And His Spirit lives inside you! Don't be afraid. God's got you, friend!

> Jesus, thank You for being right next to me in everything I do. Thank You that I never have to be afraid.

FORGETTING THE PAST

Let us keep looking to Jesus. Our faith comes from
Him and He is the One Who makes it perfect.
HEBREWS 12:2 NLV

. . . .

You've probably made some mistakes in your life, right? Who hasn't? Like all of us, you might have some embarrassing things in your past that you'd really like to forget. But you don't have to let those memories steal your joy or make you afraid of the future. Isaiah 43:18–19 (NLV) says, "Do not remember the things that have happened before. Do not think about the things of the past. See, I will do a new thing. It will begin happening now."

Jesus doesn't want you to keep carrying old burdens around. You can't fix everything, and you certainly can't fix other people. But you can fix your mind on Christ!

Philippians 3:13–14 (NIV) reminds us, "Forgetting what is behind and straining toward what is ahead, I press on toward the goal to win the prize for which God has called me heavenward in Christ Jesus."

Jesus, please help me let go of past failures that
steal my joy. I choose to fix my mind on You.

GOD IS ALWAYS WITH YOU

God has said, "I will never leave you or let you be alone."
HEBREWS 13:5 NLV

. . . .

No one is completely faithful all the time. That is, except Jesus. Humans are just that—human. We mess up. We make mistakes. We get it wrong sometimes. But God never does. He is faithful all the time! And He directs all His love and faithfulness right toward you.

God will never forget you. He'll never give up on you. He'll never lie to you. He'll never ever stop loving you. Nothing you could ever do will change His mind about how much He loves you. God looks at you and smiles because He sees Jesus in you. You are covered in His righteousness (2 Corinthians 5:21).

That is some powerful encouragement right there! Remember, you were made for more than a dull and boring life. God has you on a grand adventure, and He is right there with you every step of the way.

Father God, I'm so thankful that I'm always on Your mind and that You always keep Your promises to me.

MIRACLES THEN AND NOW

Jesus Christ is the same yesterday and today and forever.
HEBREWS 13:8 NLV

What does God's Word tell us about Jesus today? He is the same yesterday, today, and forever. That means that God's miracles you've heard about from the Bible are still possible today. Anything He has done before, He can do again.

What miracles do you remember hearing about from the Bible? Can you list some of them? God parted the Red Sea right down the middle so that His people could escape from Egypt. Jesus changed water into wine and healed many sick people. He made enough food for thousands of people to eat out of five loaves of bread and two fish. What else do you remember? Do you believe God can still work those kinds of miracles today? Of course He can! Ask God to help your faith grow.

> Lord God, I'm so glad to know that You never change. You are still all-powerful and able to do anything. Thank You for Your miracles. Open my mind and heart to believe in them still.

SHARING WITH OTHERS

*And do not forget to do good and to share with
others, for with such sacrifices God is pleased.*
HEBREWS 13:16 NIV

God wants us to share and have a generous heart. Even if you don't have much to share, you can bless someone with whatever you do have. Being willing to share means more than just being willing to share your things.

God has blessed you with special gifts and talents that only you have. God wants to use you to bless others with those gifts He's given you.

Gifts that come from your heart mean a lot more to people than "stuff" in the long run, anyway, especially when they're for your family members or close friends. Grandmas and grandpas love getting homemade gifts. Moms and dads treasure the things you make for them. And who wouldn't love to have a special dessert made by you or a chore done for them? There are lots and lots of things you can share, even if you don't have a penny!

Father God, thanks for the gifts You've given me.
Show me ways that I can share them with others.

JOY DURING TROUBLE

Dear brothers and sisters, when troubles of any kind come your way, consider it an opportunity for great joy. For you know that when your faith is tested, your endurance has a chance to grow. So let it grow, for when your endurance is fully developed, you will be perfect and complete, needing nothing.
JAMES 1:2–4 NLT

• •

Consider problems as opportunities for joy? Did today's scripture passage really just say that? How are we supposed to do that? I hope you're learning that you'll never be able to see problems in a positive light on your own. But you *can* do it in the strength and power of Jesus!

Troubles and hard things are an everyday part of living here in our world. We aren't in heaven yet, and life can never be perfect here on earth until Jesus comes back.

But with the power of God's Spirit at work in us, we can remember that God is good. We can trust His faithfulness. We can practice His presence and peace during each moment.

Lord, I believe You hold the whole universe in
Your hands. I know You're working things out
for my good, so I trust You even in hard times.
Please fill me with Your joy no matter what.

ASK GOD!

*If you do not have wisdom, ask God for it. He is always ready
to give it to you and will never say you are wrong for asking.*
JAMES 1:5 NLV

· ·

New followers of Jesus need wisdom. And all you have to do is ask
for it! As a girl who is made for more, you'll recognize your need for
wisdom every day of your life. Need help with school? Ask God! Need
help with friends? Ask God! Need help having patience with your little
brother? Ask God!

God has all the answers to absolutely everything. He is happy to
help you and give you wisdom. He doesn't want you to be confused.
He wants you to trust Him to help you when you need it. Be listening
for His voice, and He will give you the answers you seek. Sometimes
you'll hear His direct answer in His Word, in a book like this, in a song,
or in any other way God wants to speak to you.

Get in the habit of asking God for help in everything.

Thanks for giving me wisdom, Lord. You have
all the answers. Remind me that You are here
for me in every problem and situation.

157

LET'S WORSHIP

Every good and perfect gift is from above, coming down from the Father of the heavenly lights, who does not change like shifting shadows.

JAMES 1:17 NIV

. . . .

The Lord is the God of the Old Testament and the New. He was powerful then and He is still all-powerful today. He never changes. All the miracles He has done in the past, He is still capable of today. And every good gift is from Him.

First Chronicles 29:10–13 (MSG) says, "Blessed are you, GOD of Israel, our father from of old and forever. To you, O GOD, belong the greatness and the might, the glory, the victory, the majesty, the splendor; yes! Everything in heaven, everything on earth; the kingdom all yours! You've raised yourself high over all. Riches and glory come from you, you're ruler over all; you hold strength and power in the palm of your hand to build up and strengthen all. And here we are, O God, our God, giving thanks to you, praising your splendid Name."

Isn't that a cool prayer of worship?

Lord, I just want to worship
You today. You are awesome!

HEAR AND OBEY

Obey the Word of God. If you hear only and do not act, you are only fooling yourself. Anyone who hears the Word of God and does not obey is like a man looking at his face in a mirror. After he sees himself and goes away, he forgets what he looks like.
JAMES 1:22–24 NLV

God has a good sense of humor. He created laughter, after all. Imagine looking at yourself in the mirror and then completely forgetting what you look like as soon as you walk away. How silly would that be? God likes to explain things to us in ways that we understand. He's the best teacher and He uses funny things to get our attention sometimes.

He says that if you hear His Word and don't do what it says, you're just like the person who looks in a mirror and then forgets what she looks like. Instead, God wants us to know His Word and let our actions match what we've heard from God.

Ask God for help in knowing and doing His Word.

Lord, please help me to be a good listener and to put into action everything that I hear from You.

LOOKING FOR WISDOM

But the wisdom that comes from heaven is first of all pure. Then it gives peace. It is gentle and willing to obey. It is full of loving-kindness and of doing good. It has no doubts and does not pretend to be something it is not.
JAMES 3:17 NLV

• •

These days, when grown-ups and teens need answers, they often go to Google. But the answers they find are rarely pure, peaceful, or good. You might find the answer you're looking for, but it will be mixed with thousands of opinions and you have to sift through a bunch of junk to find some truth. And God made you for more! So instead of doing what everyone else is doing, learn to go to God first right now while you're still young. He will bless you for it!

When you need wisdom, the Bible says that you can ask God for it and He'll give it to you—just because you asked Him (James 1:5)! You never have to sift through any questionable content to find wisdom from God. He will give you pure answers that promote peace and love.

*Father God, when I need wisdom and answers,
help me to learn to come to You first.*

ASK AND RECEIVE

You do not have because you do not ask God.
JAMES 4:2 NIV

A lot of times we forget to bring things to God first. We try to get our needs met from other people and other things when God is just waiting for us to come to Him.

In Luke 11:9–10 (NIV) Jesus says, "Ask and it will be given to you; seek and you will find; knock and the door will be opened to you. For everyone who asks receives; the one who seeks finds; and to the one who knocks, the door will be opened."

We can ask God for anything. He wants us to talk to Him about every single thing. He wants to walk with us and have a real relationship with us. Is He going to give us every little thing we ask for? Probably not. But He will give us everything we need. And as we come to Him in prayer, He changes our hearts to be more like His.

Lord, please help me to come to You first with all my wants and needs. I know You want to help.

THE POWER OF PRAYER

*Therefore confess your sins to each other and pray
for each other so that you may be healed. The prayer
of a righteous person is powerful and effective.*
JAMES 5:16 NIV

Prayer is very powerful. The Bible tells us so! The Amplified Bible explains this verse a bit more. Check it out: "The heartfelt and persistent prayer of a righteous man (believer) can accomplish much [when put into action and made effective by God—it is dynamic and can have tremendous power]."

Your prayers can accomplish a lot! Not only do we get to know God better when we talk with Him, but our prayers can make things happen. God's Word tells us to pray for others so that they can be healed. This means not only that physical bodies can be healed but also that broken hearts can be mended. Do you know anyone who is sad or lonely? Anyone who has an illness or cancer? Pray for them! They matter to Jesus.

Thank You that my prayers matter to You,
Lord! I pray for my friends and family who
need Your powerful healing in their lives.

YOUR INHERITANCE

All praise to God, the Father of our Lord Jesus Christ. It is by his great mercy that we have been born again, because God raised Jesus Christ from the dead. Now we live with great expectation, and we have a priceless inheritance— an inheritance that is kept in heaven for you, pure and undefiled, beyond the reach of change and decay.
1 PETER 1:3–4 NLT

Wealthy families leave an inheritance for their children. All of their earthly possessions get passed to someone else when they die because—as you probably know—you can't take anything with you! Kings and queens pass their fortunes and crowns down to their children, and God does the same for you through the death and resurrection of Jesus!

If you have trusted Christ as your Savior, you have been born again as a daughter of the High King! You're His princess and He keeps your inheritance safe in heaven for all eternity. Now you can live the rest of your life with great expectation, knowing what awaits you in heaven!

Lord God, I love that You're my Father—and that makes me a daughter of the King! I will follow You all the days of my life, expecting that all Your dreams for me will come true.

GOD'S PRINCESS

*You are a chosen people. You are royal priests, a holy
nation, God's very own possession. As a result, you
can show others the goodness of God, for he called
you out of the darkness into his wonderful light.*
1 PETER 2:9 NLT

Can you picture yourself walking before your King? You are His
princess. Imagine what it's like to be in the courts of heaven, in the
throne room of God.

Ephesians 3:12 (NIV) says, "In him and through faith in him we may
approach God with freedom and confidence." This is all because of
Jesus and the price He paid to rescue you from darkness, redeem you
from sin, and release you from all anxiety and fear.

In the courts of heaven, you have a place of high honor. God will
receive you with delight because He loves you so much. Nothing you
could ever think or do will change that. All because of Jesus. Believe it.

Lord, I'm continually amazed at the truth of
who You are and who I am because of You. Help
me to be a humble and kind princess. I want to
share Your love and goodness with everyone.

BLESSING YOUR BODY

*Do not let your beauty come from the outside. It should not
be the way you comb your hair or the wearing of gold or the
wearing of fine clothes. Your beauty should come from the
inside. It should come from the heart. This is the kind that lasts.
Your beauty should be a gentle and quiet spirit. In God's sight
this is of great worth and no amount of money can buy it.*
1 PETER 3:3–4 NLV

• •

Do you ever wish you were created a little differently? Maybe with straight hair or smoother skin? God wants you to know that you are beautiful just the way you are!

Get in front of a mirror. Start at your feet and work your way up. Thank God for feet that get you where you need to go. Thank Him for your legs that are strong. Thank Him for arms to hug your family and friends. Thank Him specifically for every part of your amazing body.

Ask God to continue blessing your body with health and strength.

*Lord, thank You for my body. Help me
to accept myself just the way I am.*

USiNG YOUR GiFTS
FOR GOD'S KiNGDOM

God has given each of you a gift. Use it to help
each other. This will show God's loving-favor.
1 PETER 4:10 NLV

. . . .

Have you figured out some of the things you're really good at? Do you know what gifts and talents God gave you? Practice getting even better at those gifts because God wants to use them in special ways to bring Him glory and to bring others into His kingdom. Aren't you amazed at the ways God can use us to bless the people around us?

First Timothy 4:14 reminds us not to neglect the gifts God has given us. In other words, don't forget about your gifts! Never stop working on them or practicing them or using them!

God has big plans and a glorious adventure for your life—and He intends to use those special gifts He has given you.

Lord, use my gifts the way You
want to. I choose to follow You.

YOUR DAILY CHALLENGE

Dear friends, your faith is going to be tested as if it were going through fire. Do not be surprised at this. Be happy that you are able to share some of the suffering of Christ. When His shining-greatness is shown, you will be filled with much joy.
1 PETER 4:12–13 NLV

Jesus Himself told us we're going to have trouble here on earth, so we should expect it. Remember that He also said, "Take heart! I have overcome the world" (John 16:33 NIV).

But how can we live with joy in our hearts while we're anticipating trouble? Well, we wake up each morning expecting some challenges, and we ask Jesus to help us through each one. We don't have to be sad or afraid, expecting the worst.

Always look at trouble as a challenge that can be conquered with the power and love of Jesus.

Jesus, I know I'm going to have some problems today. But instead of getting grumpy or being afraid, I will take Your hand and let You help me through this day.

FISHERMAN PRAYERS

*Humble yourselves, therefore, under the mighty hand of
God so that at the proper time he may exalt you, casting
all your anxieties on him, because he cares for you.*
1 PETER 5:6–7 ESV

• •

Think of a fisherman who casts his line into the water. Now imagine doing that with a big worry of yours stuck to the end of the hook. Can you let it go? How many times do you cast a worry on Jesus in prayer and then reel it right back in?

Today's scripture in the Amplified Bible reads this way: "Casting all your cares [all your anxieties, all your worries, and all your concerns, once and for all] on Him, for He cares about you [with deepest affection, and watches over you very carefully]."

Do you really believe that Jesus cares about you with deepest affection? Do you trust that He's actually watching over you very carefully? If you do, then you can cast your line into the water and leave your worries with Jesus.

Jesus, please increase my faith. Help me let go
of my worries and trust You with everything.

STAND AGAINST THE ENEMY

*Keep awake! Watch at all times. The devil is working
against you. He is walking around like a hungry lion
with his mouth open. He is looking for someone to eat.
Stand against him and be strong in your faith.*
1 PETER 5:8–9 NLV

• •

Even though the enemy knows he has already been defeated by Jesus, he's still trying his best to get into your head and discourage you so you won't be able to live well for Jesus. That's why Jesus wants you to stay alert.

Don't fall for Satan's tricks, because he is the father of lies (John 8:44). You have power in the name of Jesus to get rid of any evil you come up against. You don't have to be afraid, just alert. Don't focus on the frightfulness of the enemy. Focus on Jesus and His power to fight your battles! Be encouraged by this verse: "So give yourselves to God. Stand against the devil and he will run away from you" (James 4:7 NLV).

*Lord, help me to stay alert and not fall for any
of the enemy's tricks. Thank You that You are
greater than any evil I will ever come against.*

169

EVERYTHING YOU NEED

He gives us everything we need for life and for holy living. He gives it through His great power. As we come to know Him better, we learn that He called us to share His own shining-greatness and perfect life.
2 PETER 1:3 NLV

• •

God's Word says that He has given you everything you need to live a life that is honoring to Him. Did you catch that? He has given you everything you need! Everything that God wants you to have and to know right now is currently available to you.

You don't have to wait until you go to church or finish school or get home from camp. You don't need to worry about having all of the answers for the future. You have everything you need to be close to God right now! You are free to be yourself and live the life God created you to live.

Jesus, I can't thank You enough for giving me everything I need to be close to You in each moment. Because of Your divine power, I am free to love You and be loved by You without worry.

LEARNING TO SAY NO

*Do your best to add holy living to your faith. Then add
to this a better understanding. As you have a better
understanding, be able to say no when you need to. Do not
give up. And as you wait and do not give up, live God-like.*
2 PETER 1:5–6 NLV

· ·

The New International Version puts 2 Peter 1:5–7 this way: "For this
very reason, make every effort to add to your faith goodness; and
to goodness, knowledge; and to knowledge, self-control; and to
self-control, perseverance; and to perseverance, godliness; and to
godliness, mutual affection; and to mutual affection, love." That's
quite a list! But as the fruits of God's Spirit grow inside of you, these
values come along too.

Sometimes it's hard to have self-control and say no (especially
when there happen to be fresh cookies close by!). But paying attention to your body and saying no when you need to is very important.
This kind of self-control will help you stay safe and healthy in many
different situations as you grow up.

Lord, I want to learn how to pay more
attention to what my body is telling me.
Please grow the fruit of self-control in me.

STEADY AND STRONG

The Lord is not slow about keeping His promise as some people think. He is waiting for you. The Lord does not want any person to be punished forever. He wants all people to be sorry for their sins and turn from them.
2 Peter 3:9 nlv

The Bible tells us that Jesus is coming back for all of us who love Him so that we can be with Him forever. James 5:7–8 (msg) says, "Meanwhile, friends, wait patiently for the Master's Arrival. . . . Stay steady and strong. The Master could arrive at any time."

Many people wonder why Jesus hasn't come back already and removed all the bad things from this world. The Bible has an answer for that. God loves us deeply and wants everyone to trust Him. So He is patient, giving people more time than they deserve to make a choice for Christ.

While we wait for His return, God wants us to be steady and strong in our faith.

Father God, please help me to be steady and strong as I wait for Your return. Help me share Your love with friends and family who need to know about You.

SPOTLESS AND BLAMELESS

Dear friends, since you are waiting for these
things to happen, do all you can to be found by
Him in peace. Be clean and free from sin.
2 PETER 3:14 NLV

The New International Version translates this verse, "Make every effort to be found spotless, blameless and at peace with him."

Being spotless and blameless sounds like such an impossible task, doesn't it? That's because it is. There is absolutely no way you can keep yourself spotless and blameless in your own strength. If you could, you wouldn't need Jesus, right?

But God tells us that what is impossible with us is possible with Him (Luke 18:27)! When God looks at you, He sees you as spotless and blameless because Jesus took all of your sin and made you perfectly clean. The only way you can live a spotless and blameless life in this confusing world is in the power of Jesus Christ Himself. He's the One at work in you.

Lord God, I know there is no way I can be spotless
and blameless on my own. I'm so thankful that
You see me as clean and pure because of Jesus.

LOVE AND LIGHT

*This is what we heard Him tell us. We are passing it on to you.
God is light. There is no darkness in Him. If we say we are joined
together with Him but live in darkness, we are telling a lie. We
are not living the truth. If we live in the light as He is in the light,
we share what we have in God with each other. And the blood
of Jesus Christ, His Son, makes our lives clean from all sin.*
1 JOHN 1:5–7 NLV

The apostle John wrote the book of 1 John to encourage all believers in their faith. John was one of Jesus' disciples, so he walked and talked with Jesus. He saw Jesus' miracles firsthand. He heard exactly what Jesus said during His times of teaching. The book of 1 John really helps us understand the love of Jesus and our purpose as we carry His love and light out into the world.

Lord Jesus, thank You for lighting up my life with Your love. Help me to walk with You in the light all the days of my life. I know I was made for that!

WHEN YOU MESS UP

If we tell Him our sins, He is faithful and we can depend on Him
to forgive us of our sins. He will make our lives clean from all sin.
1 JOHN 1:9 NLV

. . . .

As humans, we make big mistakes from time to time. When we confess our sins to Jesus and receive His forgiveness, the next step is for us to turn away from the sin we've been doing. He already knows what you've done, but He wants to talk with you about it. He wants to help you through it and give you peace. We can't pretend it will just go away on its own. It takes action on our part.

When you've messed up big, turn back to Jesus and start to trust Him again—really trust Him. When you trust Jesus with everything you have, He gives you the ability to do good and to be faithful. Remember, His power is alive and at work within you.

Jesus, thank You for Your grace and forgiveness
in my life when I mess up. I want to do Your
will and bring glory and honor to You.

LAVISH LOVE

See what great love the Father has for us that He
would call us His children. And that is what we are.
For this reason the people of the world do not know
who we are because they did not know Him.
1 JOHN 3:1 NLV

The New International Version translates today's verse, "See what great love the Father has lavished on us, that we should be called children of God! And that is what we are!"

There is such great joy in knowing that the God of the universe knows us personally and loves us lavishly. To lavish means "to give without limit." If you remember nothing else about God, remember this: God loves you without limit! Remember this truth when you wake up and start your day. Thank Him for His love as you eat your breakfast. Share His love with everyone you see today with a smile or a kind word.

God says, "I love you!" Can you hear Him?

Father God, thank You for Your lavish love.
I can't begin to understand how You can
know everything about me and still love
me without limit! I love You so much!

SEEING JESUS

Dear friends, we are already God's children, but he has not yet shown us what we will be like when Christ appears. But we do know that we will be like him, for we will see him as he really is. And all who have this eager expectation will keep themselves pure, just as he is pure.
1 JOHN 3:2–3 NLT

Soon we will be able to see Jesus as He really is. Can you imagine actually seeing Jesus for the first time? The Bible tells us about amazing things that will happen to us in the end times. While we wait for Jesus to return, God wants us to be pure, like He is. But remember, we can't do this on our own.

The Bible says that if you are a follower of Jesus, you are being transformed into His likeness day by day (2 Corinthians 3:17–18). His Spirit comes into your life and changes you, keeping you pure for what is to come.

Jesus, thank You for Your Spirit who is always at work in my heart. Thank You that I don't have to be afraid or worried that I have to keep myself pure and spotless all on my own. I'm Yours, Jesus!

WHAT YOU NEED TO KNOW ABOUT YOUR ENEMY

*But when people keep on sinning, it shows that they belong
to the devil, who has been sinning since the beginning. But
the Son of God came to destroy the works of the devil.*
1 JOHN 3:8 NLT

Satan is a liar, so he might try to get you to believe that he is way more powerful than he is. When you're scared or facing something that comes from the enemy, call out to Jesus and let Him handle it. Don't focus on your fears; focus on Jesus.

Here's what you need to know about the enemy:

- Satan is real (John 10:10; 1 Peter 5:8).
- He is a liar (John 8:44) and sometimes pretends to be good (2 Corinthians 11:14).
- He tries to lead us away from Jesus (2 Corinthians 11:3).
- Greater is Jesus' power in you than the enemy's (1 John 4:4).
- Jesus protects you with His armor (Ephesians 6:10–18).
- You are safe from the devil when you trust in Jesus (James 4:7).

Jesus, thank You for Your protection from the enemy.
I know You are more powerful than any tricks he
might try to play on me. I am safe with You.

LOVE YOUR ENEMIES

My children, let us not love with words or in talk only. Let us love by what we do and in truth.
1 JOHN 3:18 NLV

You probably don't have too many enemies at your age, but the Bible says that some people will hate you just because you believe in God. Don't let this keep you from telling others that you love God! The important thing is to show them that you love God. Our actions speak a lot louder than our words.

People can spot a fake a mile away. So if you're going to love someone, do it with all your heart—with your actions. Pray for God to change any false motives that might be in you so you do good to others without expecting anything in return.

Luke 6:35 (NIV) says, "But love your enemies, do good to them, and lend to them without expecting to get anything back. Then your reward will be great, and you will be children of the Most High, because he is kind to the ungrateful and wicked."

Lord God, sometimes it's hard to love people who aren't very nice. Please give me Your supernatural strength to show Your love to others.

TRUST JESUS AND LOVE EACH OTHER

This is what He said we must do: Put your trust in the name of His Son, Jesus Christ, and love each other. Christ told us to do this. The person who obeys Christ lives by the help of God and God lives in him. We know He lives in us by the Holy Spirit He has given us.
1 JOHN 3:23–24 NLV

God gave us His Word so we would know Him and know how to follow Him. *The Message* paraphrases today's scripture passage this way: "As we keep his commands, we live deeply and surely in him, and he lives in us. And this is how we experience his deep and abiding presence in us: by the Spirit he gave us."

What a fun adventure to get to know Jesus and watch the Word of God come alive in your heart! Be on the lookout for the miraculous ways you start remembering God's Word at just the right time. That's one of the ways the Holy Spirit works inside you!

Lord, I'm starting to understand that following You isn't a complicated thing. You've made it pretty simple: trust You and love others. Thanks for giving me Your Spirit to help me do that!

ALWAYS CHECK IT OUT

Dear Christian friends, do not believe every spirit.
But test the spirits to see if they are from God for
there are many false preachers in the world.
1 JOHN 4:1 NLV

. . . .

The Message puts 1 John 4:1 this way: "Don't believe everything you hear. Carefully weigh and examine what people tell you. Not everyone who talks about God comes from God."

Remember that the enemy likes to trick people. And he's really good at it. He likes to deceive, and the Bible says that he even disguises himself as an angel of light (2 Corinthians 11:14).

Some people who have been tricked like to take certain verses out of the Bible and make them say what they want them to say. So always test what people say about God with His Word. Look it up. Get a study Bible and find out what God's Word really says. Ask wise grown-ups for help.

You have the Spirit of God living inside your heart, so if someone says something about God and it doesn't seem quite right, check it out.

Lord God, please give me wisdom about You.
Thank You that I have Your Spirit to guide me.

THE POWER INSIDE YOU

My children, you are a part of God's family. You have stood against these false preachers and had power over them. You had power over them because the One Who lives in you is stronger than the one who is in the world.
1 JOHN 4:4 NLV

. . . .

The New International Version says it this way: "The one who is in you is greater than the one who is in the world." This is a powerful verse that is great to remember and say out loud whenever you're feeling afraid. Take a minute right now to write down this verse on a sticky note or a piece of construction paper. Ask the Holy Spirit to help you memorize it. Place it somewhere you'll see it every day.

With God's power alive and at work in you, you have nothing to be afraid of. Give thanks to God that He is with you always.

Thanks for being with me all the time, Jesus, and for caring about the fact that I'm young. You've given me everything I need to live for You, including truths to remember when I'm afraid.

HOW DO I LOVE GOD?

God has shown His love to us by sending His only Son into the world. God did this so we might have life through Christ.
1 JOHN 4:9 NLV

• •

Sometimes it's hard to know how to love God back after such a huge sacrifice. His great love can be overwhelming! How could we ever pay Him back? Well, we can't. But when we follow God's Word, listen for His voice, and love others, we are showing our love for God.

In John 14:15 (NIV) Jesus says, "If you love me, keep my commands." He wants us to listen and obey.

But what about those times when we're not sure if we're loving God very well? "We know and rely on the love God has for us" (1 John 4:16 NIV). The only way we can love at all is because He loved us first. He is the author of love, and He'll continue to show us how to love better and better as we follow Him.

Father God, please help me to listen for Your voice in my life and to follow after You, relying on the love You have for me.

JESUS LOVES YOU

This is love! It is not that we loved God but that He loved us.
For God sent His Son to pay for our sins with His own blood.
1 JOHN 4:10 NLV

• •

Look at these amazing verses that show how much God loves you:

- "The Lord came to us from far away, saying, 'I have loved you with a love that lasts forever. So I have helped you come to Me with loving-kindness'" (Jeremiah 31:3 NLV).
- "But God showed His love to us. While we were still sinners, Christ died for us" (Romans 5:8 NLV).
- "No one can have greater love than to give his life for his friends" (John 15:13 NLV).

And those are just a few! There are a ton more.

Nothing will change the fact that God loves you. Nothing you can ever do will cause Him to love you any more or less than He already does.

Jesus, I accept Your great love for me! I believe
You died on the cross to show me Your love and to
take away all my sin. Forgive me for my mistakes. I
know I can't make good choices without Your help.
I choose to follow You. Help me be like You, Jesus.

WITH ALL YOUR HEART

*If anyone acknowledges that Jesus is the Son of
God, God lives in them and they in God.*
1 JOHN 4:15 NIV

. . . .

John wrote the letter of 1 John to early Christians who had gotten off track. They were trying too hard to fit in with people who didn't know Jesus. Sounds familiar, right? That's because God's Word is living and active and still very much applies to us today. John and the other followers of Jesus had developed a close relationship with God through Jesus. John reminds us that this relationship is possible for all of us.

God wants you to know Him personally! You can embrace Him with all of your heart. You can do that by listening for Jesus and getting to know His voice—that gentle voice that encourages and comforts you.

Ask God to make Himself known to you, and He will. . .if you're listening.

*Lord God, please help me get to know Your voice.
I want to love You with all of my heart. Lead
me as I grow up knowing and following You.*

BIGGER THAN YOUR FEAR

There is no fear in love. Perfect love puts fear out of our hearts. People have fear when they are afraid of being punished. The man who is afraid does not have perfect love.
1 JOHN 4:18 NLV

. . . .

A lot of people are afraid of things. But some people actually live their lives in fear. You see these people every day, but you might not know what they struggle with on the inside. They are at church, at school, and at the mall. They might even say they follow God, but their lives show more fear than faith. These people fear the future and anything unknown.

But the Bible says that we can live our lives without any fear! God's perfect love actually throws fear out of our hearts. Jesus wants us to come to Him with the faith of a child (Matthew 19:14), believing that God is bigger than anything we could ever face. Even in the scariest situation we could imagine, God is bigger!

Father God, thank You that You are with
me and that I never have to be afraid.

LOVE WITHOUT FEAR

We love Him because He loved us first.
1 JOHN 4:19 NLV

. . . .

God is not angry with you. He sees you through the love and sacrifice of Jesus, so you can always approach Him without fear! A person who is afraid of God's punishment doesn't understand who they are in Christ. Remember yesterday's verse said, "There is no fear in love, but perfect love casts out fear. For fear has to do with punishment, and whoever fears has not been perfected in love" (1 John 4:18 ESV).

You don't have to work harder or be a better Christian to earn God's love. When you begin to believe who you are in Christ, it changes everything. You start living differently. You realize how deeply loved you are, and this awareness sets you free.

As Jesus pours His love into your life, it spills over into the lives of those around you.

You loved me first, Lord. That's how I
know what love is. I'm so thankful I am
welcomed and loved in Your presence.

YOU CAN KNOW FOR SURE

I have written these things to you who believe in the name of the Son of God. Now you can know you have life that lasts forever.
1 JOHN 5:13 NLV

. . . .

You can know for sure that you are a child of God. John wanted to make sure all believers knew that. Jesus loves you and came to save you forever.

Take a look at these verses from Psalms:

"Because he set his love on Me, therefore I will save him; I will set him [securely] on high, because he knows My name [he confidently trusts and relies on Me, knowing I will never abandon him, no, never]. He will call upon Me, and I will answer him; I will be with him in trouble; I will rescue him and honor him. With a long life I will satisfy him and I will let him see My salvation." (Psalm 91:14–16 AMP)

As a precious daughter of the King, you are treasured in God's eyes. You can trust His promises to you. He will never abandon you, no, never!

Lord, thank You that I can know for sure that I'm saved. Thank You for Your eternal love for me.

THE FRUIT OF GOODNESS

We know that no child of God keeps on sinning. The Son of God watches over him and the devil cannot get near him.
1 JOHN 5:18 NLV

. . . .

It's hard to make good choices all the time, right? We definitely need God's help with that! We can stay away from sin and make good choices because Jesus protects us from the enemy and helps us turn away from evil.

Psalm 37:3 (NLV) tells us to "trust in the Lord, and do good." The Spirit of God grows the spiritual fruit of goodness inside of us (see Galatians 5:22–23) when we turn to Him for help with our choices. We all make mistakes sometimes. When this happens, God wants us to run to Him for help instead of running away. He isn't mad at you. He wants to show you His love and help you make better choices next time.

Lord, thank You for Your forgiveness when
I mess up. I'm so thankful You love me
and want to help me make better choices.
Please grow goodness in my heart.

STAYING FAITHFUL

*Loving-favor and loving-kindness and peace are ours as we live
in truth and love. These come from God the Father and from the
Lord Jesus Christ, Who is the Son of the Father. . . . Love means
that we should live by obeying His Word. From the beginning
He has said in His Word that our hearts should be full of love.*
2 JOHN 1:3, 6 NLV

Second John is a tiny little book in the back of the Bible written to
the church and all of us who follow Jesus, so that we would trust
the Gospel and learn to love one another. John warns against false
teachers who may sound like believers but are actually turning people
away from the truth.

As you grow up, you're going to face situations just like this. Ask
Jesus to help you stay faithful to His love and to His Word. He will
help you.

> Jesus, You have my heart. I want to know the
> truth about You and about me. Protect my
> mind and my heart as I grow up. Please keep
> me close to You and help me to stay faithful.

GOSPEL TRUTH

Dear friend, you are doing a good work by being kind to the Christians, and for sure, to the strangers. They have told the church about your love. It will be good for you to help them on their way as God would have you.
3 JOHN 1:5–6 NLV

- -

Third John is another tiny letter written by John to talk about some important things. God wants believers to take care of each other by showing love and hospitality. Hospitality is the way you treat other people, friends or strangers, especially when they are in your home.

John also warns about a guy who was a church leader but was making some bad choices. Verse 11 (NLV) says, "Dear friend, do not follow what is sinful, but follow what is good. The person who does what is good belongs to God. The person who does what is sinful has not seen God."

Someone who keeps sinning over and over and doesn't repent isn't following God. The Gospel of Jesus is the truth. You were made to know Him and love Him.

Jesus, I'm so thankful You've chosen me to be Your daughter. Help me share Your truth with anyone You ask me to.

STRONG IN FAITH

I am writing to you who have been chosen by God the Father. You are kept for Jesus Christ. May you have much of God's loving-kindness and peace and love. Dear friends, I have been trying to write to you about what God did for us when He saved us from the punishment of sin. Now I must write to you and tell you to fight hard for the faith which was once and for all given to the holy people of God.

JUDE 1:1–3 NLV

. . . .

The book of Jude is believed to have been written by Jesus' half brother. It's a pretty short book too—only one chapter. But it is packed with goodness and it's a great book for a girl who is made for more to spend some time in!

Jude encourages us all to be strong in the faith and to stay close to God.

Lord, I'm thankful for Your Word that guides me along Your way. I am "kept for Jesus," and that amazing truth makes my heart sing for joy! Give me strength to keep the faith, no matter what arrows come my way.

STAY iN LOVE

*Keep yourselves in the love of God. Wait for life that lasts
forever through the loving-kindness of our Lord Jesus Christ.*
JUDE 1:21 NLV

• •

This scripture from Jude reminds us to keep ourselves in the love of God. Doing this requires a choice and an action on our part. It doesn't involve mustering our own strength but rather taking our thoughts captive and making them obedient to Christ.

Remember what "taking our thoughts captive" means? Here's a simple breakdown: when you have a negative thought, you take it to Jesus immediately and allow Him to remind you of His love for you and His truth.

John 15:9–11 (NLV) says, "I have loved you just as My Father has loved Me. Stay in My love. If you obey My teaching, you will live in My love. In this way, I have obeyed My Father's teaching and live in His love. I have told you these things so My joy may be in you and your joy may be full."

Lord, please change my heart and my
thoughts to match Your loving truth.

GOD IS ABLE

There is One Who can keep you from falling and can bring you before Himself free from all sin. He can give you great joy as you stand before Him in His shining-greatness. He is the only God. He is the One Who saves from the punishment of sin through Jesus Christ our Lord. May He have shining-greatness and honor and power and the right to do all things. He had this before the world began, He has it now, and He will have this forever. Let it be so.
JUDE 1:24–25 NLV

. . . .

Do you believe God is able to be and do and provide everything you need? Talk to Jesus about this in prayer. Bring your thoughts, feelings, and doubts to God. He can handle all of your honesty. Allow Him access to align your thoughts and feelings with His truth. What does He want you to know?

Let this scripture from 2 Corinthians be your encouragement today: "And God is able to bless you abundantly, so that in all things at all times, having all that you need, you will abound in every good work" (9:8 NIV).

Lord God, I need You to strengthen my faith. I want to believe You are able.

JESUS IS COMING SOON

John tells that the Word of God is true. He tells of Jesus Christ and all that he saw and heard of Him. The man who reads this Book and listens to it being read and obeys what it says will be happy. For all these things will happen soon.
REVELATION 1:2–3 NLV

John wrote the book of Revelation, and it is the last book in the Bible. Turning to this book and starting to read it can be a little overwhelming. It's a serious book, but it is also very hopeful! It talks about the last days and what things will be like when Jesus comes back.

You don't have to fear, because you are God's child. Your name is written in the book of life, and Jesus is preparing a place for you in heaven.

While you wait for these end-times things to take place, keep on loving Jesus and listening for His voice. He will give you the courage to share His love with others so that they may have eternal life with Jesus too.

Jesus, thank You that I don't have to fear the future. You are going to take me with You to Your perfect place.

JESUS IS THE FIRST AND THE LAST

The Lord God says, "I am the First and the Last, the beginning and the end of all things. I am the All-powerful One Who was and Who is and Who is to come."
REVELATION 1:8 NLV

· ·

What are the first and last letters of our alphabet? A and Z, right? Well, the first letter of the Greek alphabet is called Alpha. The New International Version says, " 'I am the Alpha and the Omega,' says the Lord God, 'who is, and who was, and who is to come, the Almighty' " (Revelation 1:8).

Guess what the last letter of the Greek alphabet is called? Did you guess Omega? If so, you're right. Jesus is the Alpha and Omega. He says He is the first and the last, the beginning and the end. He is full of love, grace, and truth and He never changes (Hebrews 13:8).

Revelation 1:17 (ESV) says, "When I saw him, I fell at his feet as though dead. But he laid his right hand on me, saying, 'Fear not, I am the first and the last.' "

Jesus, I'm so thankful that I am safe in
Your love. I will not be afraid, because
You're with me from beginning to end.

YOUR FIRST LOVE

"But I have this one thing against you. You do not love Me as you did at first. Remember how you once loved Me. Be sorry for your sin and love Me again as you did at first."
REVELATION 2:4–5 NLV

Do you remember when you first felt the love of Jesus? Picture that time in your mind. How did you feel? What did you do? The Bible warns us not to forget our first love, Jesus.

John 15:9–11 (NLV) says, "I have loved you just as My Father has loved Me. Stay in My love. If you obey My teaching, you will live in My love. In this way, I have obeyed My Father's teaching and live in His love. I have told you these things so My joy may be in you and your joy may be full."

Staying in Jesus' love means seeking Him first and talking to Him about everything. If you feel far from Jesus, tell Him you're sorry for forgetting Him. Ask Him to help you put Him first in your life.

Jesus, I'm sorry when I don't put You first in my life. Please change my heart to want to be with You more.

197

AMEN

"To the angel of the church in Laodicea write: These are the words of the Amen, the faithful and true witness, the ruler of God's creation."
REVELATION 3:14 NIV

● ●

Do you know what "amen" means? We hear it often enough—we even say it after every prayer. But have you ever wondered what it actually means?

It is most commonly used to mean "so be it" or "may it be so." You are basically stating your agreement with something. You agree that what you are hearing is "faithful and true." Amen! So be it! Those words are powerful and true.

But the Bible also tells us that Jesus Himself is the Amen! What could that possibly mean? Take a look at this little but powerful and important verse right here: "All the promises of God find their Yes in him. That is why it is through him that we utter our Amen to God for his glory" (2 Corinthians 1:20 ESV).

Jesus, You are faithful and true. God says yes to me because of You! I'm so thankful. Amen!

198

KNOCK-KNOCK

"See! I stand at the door and knock. If anyone hears My voice and opens the door, I will come in to him and we will eat together."
REVELATION 3:20 NLV

- -

Who's there? Jesus! And this is no joke! The Bible tells us we can knock on God's door and be invited in, but did you know that Jesus is knocking on your door too? Today's scripture tells us this truth.

Wouldn't the game be so easy if the person who was supposed to be hiding was actually looking for you too, whenever you play hide-and-seek? That's the really amazing thing—while we're looking for God, He's looking for us too. He wants you to find Him. He makes it pretty simple. If you look for Him, you will find Him. Remember Jeremiah 29:13 (ESV) says, "You will seek me and find me, when you seek me with all your heart."

Jesus is always knocking at the door of your heart. Will you let Him in?

Jesus, thanks for looking for me. I'm so glad You want me to find You! You've knocked on my heart and I'm letting You in.

LiKED BY GOD

*"Our Lord and our God, it is right for You to have the
shining-greatness and the honor and the power.
You made all things. They were made and have
life because You wanted it that way."*
REVELATION 4:11 NLV

• •

God created you to love you and delight in you. Just as loving parents long for children to love and enjoy, God feels this way about you. Zephaniah 3:17 (NIV) tells us: "The LORD your God is with you, the Mighty Warrior who saves. He will take great delight in you; in his love he will no longer rebuke you, but will rejoice over you with singing."

God doesn't just love you—He likes you too. The King James Version of Revelation 4:11 says, "And for thy pleasure they are and were created."

What a blessing to know that you are loved and liked and enjoyed by God Himself. Allow these thoughts to stir up praise and thankfulness in your heart.

Lord God, I praise You for caring so much for me!

PRAISING OUR HOLY GOD

Day and night they never stop saying, "Holy, holy, holy is the Lord God, the All-powerful One. He is the One Who was and Who is and Who is to come."
REVELATION 4:8 NLV

. . . .

Worship songs often praise God for being holy. Do you like to sing at home or church? Do you have a favorite worship song? Singing is one of the ways we can worship Jesus. Your praises make Jesus happy. He loves to hear His children praise Him with words and songs from their hearts.

Praising Jesus is a very powerful action. The Bible says it can even silence our enemies. Take a look: "You have taught children and infants to tell of your strength, silencing your enemies and all who oppose you" (Psalm 8:2 NLT).

The next time you are tempted to complain about something, try praising Jesus instead. Thank Him for who He is and what He's done for you. Sing to Him. You'll be amazed at how your praise silences the negative thoughts you had!

I praise You, Jesus, because of who You are. You are amazing and deserve all my worship and thanks. Thank You for giving me praise as a tool to silence the enemy!

PRAISING GOD THROUGH SCRIPTURE

*"We give thanks to you, Lord God Almighty, the
One who is and who was, because you have taken
your great power and have begun to reign."*
REVELATION 11:17 NIV

• •

Read through each of these verses about praising God. Ask Jesus what
He wants to show you. Is there something He wants you to see? What
is He saying to your heart through these scriptures?

- "Who is he, this King of glory? The Lord Almighty—he is the
  King of glory" (Psalm 24:10 NIV).
- "Restore us, God Almighty; make your face shine on us,
  that we may be saved" (Psalm 80:7 NIV).
- "LORD Almighty, blessed is the one who trusts in you" (Psalm
  84:12 NIV).
- "Who is like you, Lord God Almighty? You, LORD, are mighty,
  and your faithfulness surrounds you" (Psalm 89:8 NIV).
- "Whoever dwells in the shelter of the Most High will rest
  in the shadow of the Almighty" (Psalm 91:1 NIV).
- "I will be a Father to you, and you will be my sons and
  daughters, says the Lord Almighty" (2 Corinthians 6:18 NIV).

Jesus, You are my almighty God. You are all-powerful
and You can do anything! I believe this is true.

JESUS IS PREPARING A PLACE FOR YOU

I heard a loud voice coming from heaven. It said, "See! God's home is with men. He will live with them. They will be His people. God Himself will be with them. He will be their God."
REVELATION 21:3 NLV

. . . .

Did you know that Jesus is coming again one day? Right now, Jesus is preparing a place for you in His Father's house. (Look up John 14:1–4 to see the details!) How amazing is that? When everything is ready, He will come back for all of us who love Him.

What are we supposed to do in the meantime? Love God and love others. In Luke 12:40 (NIV) Jesus tells us, "You also must be ready, because the Son of Man will come at an hour when you do not expect him."

Jesus could return at any moment. And guess what happens then? Take a look in your Bible at Revelation 21:1–4. Here's a sneak peek at tomorrow's verse: " 'He will wipe every tear from their eyes. There will be no more death' or mourning or crying or pain. . ." (verse 4 NIV).

Jesus, thank You for the perfect plans You have for my life. I'm so grateful I get to be with You forever!

YOUR TEARS MATTER TO GOD

"God will take away all their tears. There will be no more death or sorrow or crying or pain. All the old things have passed away."
REVELATION 21:4 NLV

Does God care about the things that make you sad? Yes. Look at Psalm 56:8–9 (NLT): "You keep track of all my sorrows. You have collected all my tears in your bottle. You have recorded each one in your book. My enemies will retreat when I call to you for help. This I know: God is on my side!"

The Bible says God counts your tears and writes them down. One of Jesus' nicknames was "Man of Sorrows" because He was rejected by people (even some of His own friends) and because He was very familiar with pain and sadness. Whatever you're going through, Jesus understands because He's been there. Have you ever felt left out or not good enough for other people? Talk to God about it. Your tears matter to Him.

Lord, I'm so glad that You are with me and You care about what makes me sad. I'm so glad to know that one day there won't be any more tears or sadness!

YOUR RESERVATION IN HEAVEN

*There is no need for the sun and moon to shine
in the city. The shining-greatness of God makes
it full of light. The Lamb is its light.*
REVELATION 21:23 NLV

We don't know a whole lot about what eternity will be like because the Bible doesn't give us a ton of details. A lot of mystery surrounds what heaven will be like. But we do know this:

- There is no sun because Jesus Himself will light up the city (Revelation 21:23).
- There will be no tears or death in heaven (21:4).
- The walls and streets are made of gold (21:18, 21).
- The walls are decorated with rubies, emeralds, and other precious stones (21:19–20).
- There is plenty of space for everyone who loves Jesus (John 14:2).

Jesus has plenty of room in His house for everyone who loves and trusts Him, and He's preparing a special place just for you!

*Jesus, I'm so excited to have a reservation
in heaven for all of eternity! Thank
You for making a place for me.*

NO DARKNESS AT ALL

"I am Jesus. I have sent My angel to you with these words to the churches. I am the beginning of David and of his family. I am the bright Morning Star."
REVELATION 22:16 NLV

• •

Jesus is called the Morning Star in several places in the Bible. Take a look at this one: "We also have the prophetic message as something completely reliable, and you will do well to pay attention to it, as to a light shining in a dark place, until the day dawns and the morning star rises in your hearts" (2 Peter 1:19 NIV).

Jesus is our special light that glows in the darkness when all other lights go out. His name is all-powerful, and when He is present, the darkness must flee. You can trust that when you are in a dark and scary place, Jesus will bring the light of His presence when you call on Him for help.

First John 1:5 (NLT) says, "This is the message we heard from Jesus and now declare to you: God is light, and there is no darkness in him at all."

Jesus, You are my light. I trust You to light up the darkness when I'm afraid.

RIGHT NOW AND FOREVER

"See! I am coming soon. The one who obeys
what is written in this Book is happy!"
REVELATION 22:7 NLV

The Pharisees were the people in New Testament Bible times who thought they knew everything better than Jesus and didn't believe in Him. They asked Jesus when the kingdom of God would come. They didn't realize that through Jesus' coming to earth, the kingdom of God was already here.

Take a look: "The proud religious law-keepers asked when the holy nation of God would come. Jesus said to them, 'The holy nation of God is not coming in such a way that can be seen with the eyes' " (Luke 17:20 NLV).

The kingdom of God begins in your heart the moment you start believing in Jesus. Yes, we are waiting for Jesus to return so that we can physically be with Him forever. And yes, there will be a day when Jesus makes all things new and destroys all evil forever. But we don't have to wait for heaven to be a part of God's kingdom. It is already here.

Jesus, I'm so thankful to be a part of
Your kingdom, now and forever.

YOU MADE IT

But we have power over all these things through Jesus Who loves us so much. For I know that nothing can keep us from the love of God. Death cannot! Life cannot! Angels cannot! Leaders cannot! Any other power cannot! Hard things now or in the future cannot! The world above or the world below cannot! Any other living thing cannot keep us away from the love of God which is ours through Christ Jesus our Lord.
ROMANS 8:37–39 NLV

. . . .

We've spent quite a bit of time together going through all the books of the Bible! Our prayer is that the Holy Spirit will help these words jump to life in your heart, reminding you of God's truth when you need it, at just the right time.

God has awesome plans for your life. You are His precious daughter. You are deeply loved and valued by God. And best of all, nothing can separate you from His love! Girl, you are made for more!

Dear God, thank You for Your promises and Your truth. Please keep working in my heart as I grow up. I'm excited about all the plans You have for me.